# Read To Write

**Halsey P. Taylor**
California State Polytechnic University, Pomona

**Sheila Flume Taylor**

**Scott, Foresman and Company**

Glenview, Ill.    Dallas, Tex.    Oakland, N.J.
Palo Alto, Cal.    Tucker, Ga.    London, England

Library of Congress Cataloging in Publication Data

Main entry under title:

Read to write.

    1. College readers. 2. English language—Rhetoric.
I. Taylor, Halsey P. II. Taylor, Sheila Flume.
PE1417.R33        808'.0427        80–23797

ISBN: 0–673–15388–6

1 2 3 4 5 6 - RRC - 85 84 83 82 81 80

# Preface

We have designed *Read To Write* as an anthology for use in basic writing courses, assuming that an underlying purpose of these courses is to help students reach a point in their intellectual development at which they can express abstract ideas in writing with some clarity and ease. The book is organized developmentally, treating reading and writing as closely related, complementary skills. That is, the reading levels of the selections, the rhetorical concepts introduced in the lessons for these selections, and the writing assignments the lessons include all become increasingly challenging to students.

The book is divided into three "levels" with rhetorical categories serving as subsections within these levels. In Level One we include only those categories we think will be relatively easy for beginning students to deal with in both their reading and their writing. These are "Expression of Feeling" and the familiar category, "Description." In Level Two we repeat these categories with examples that have more depth and complexity (achieving a "spiraling" effect for reinforcement), and add two new classifications—"Narration" and "Exposition." Finally, in Level Three, we present still more challenging material in all four previously treated classifications, and we add a fifth and final one, "Persuasion." The progression throughout the book, then, is from the treatment of single-incident or single-emotion personal reminiscences through communication of specific, concrete information, to the marshaling of arguments and the presentation of abstract ideas. And within this progression we reinforce what the students have learned about reading and writing the simpler forms of communication.

For each selection there is a lesson consisting of guides for reading and understanding, vocabulary aids, a writing assignment related to the topic of the selection, and instructions for using writing techniques found in the work. The topics for writing and the rhetorical instructions that accompany them are, like the selections themselves, arranged in a spiral-developmental pattern. The selections, as well as paragraphs (in prose), and lines (in poetry), are numbered to make discussion and cross-references clearer.

Throughout the preparation of the book we have worked to include materials that will be of high interest to the students we are writing for. The selections, all of which are short, include stories, poems, and nonfiction pieces of various kinds. The topics are ones students will either be familiar with or that will attract them because of exciting action or the universal interest of the subject matter. We have chosen the selections—whether by famous or by little-known writers—primarily for their appeal to our readers and for their usefulness in helping them develop their reading and writing skills.

We are most grateful to those people who read this book in its formative stages and gave us support, helpful suggestions, and encouragement. We especially want to thank colleague John Ryan, who class-tested portions of the book in his developmental communications skills courses, and who gave valuable criticism of the book in a very early form. We appreciate the helpful reviews of John R. Dick, University of Texas, El Paso; Minnie Bruce Pratt, Fayetteville State University; Madeline Hamermesh, Normandale Community College; Alan Meyers, Truman College; Allan Danzig, City College, City University of New York; and Charles A. Moore, California State University.

We particularly want to acknowledge the encouragement and help of the people we have worked with at Scott, Foresman and Company—Paul Revenko-Jones, who showed faith in the project from the beginning, Jane Steinmann, whose perceptive editing was invaluable, and Anita Portugal, who saw the book through the production stage.

H. P. T. and S. F. T.

# Contents

# To the Student

You can read well and you can write well if you follow a few principles and practice some techniques that are available to you. We have designed this book to acquaint you with these principles and techniques and to provide you with increasingly challenging reading and writing experiences in which to use them. If you use this book consistently and thoughtfully, you will probably learn to read different kinds of material easily and with understanding. Through the reading you do here, you will learn to stretch your mind to deal with vocabulary, ideas, and forms of expression that may be new to you. These mind-stretching reading experiences, combined with your use of some writing techniques we introduce here, will help you find ways of expressing what you want to say in writing. You will learn to communicate feelings, ideas, and information in ways that satisfy you and that cause your readers to consider what you have to say.

*Read To Write,* an anthology of thirty-five short readings and related writing assignments, is divided into three levels of increasing challenge to you. Among the selections in the book, you will find stories, poems, and various kinds of nonfiction. Each selection is numbered consecutively. Within each selection paragraphs are numbered for prose, and lines are numbered for poetry. Level One consists of fairly simple selections of just two kinds: One of these we call "Expression of Feeling"; the other is labeled "Description." Level Two follows with somewhat more challenging readings in these same two categories and also with selections in two new ones, "Narration" (storytelling) and "Exposition" (presenting information). Level Three consists of more complex examples of all four of these types of readings and adds a fifth type, "Persuasion." Throughout all three levels, we have designed a writing assignment for each selection; you will find that each assignment corresponds with its accompanying selection in topic, category, and level of complexity.

You will notice throughout the book the repeated phrases "Look for," "Think about," "Write about," and "Try out." Before each selection there is a "Look for" section in which we ask you to notice —to be on the lookout for—certain key ideas and uses of language. In this section, the last item lists words that may be unfamiliar to you. It includes an informal pronunciation guide and definitions designed as quick aids to your reading. Paragraphs (or line numbers) where the term appears are set off in brackets. (For further information about any of these words, we encourage you to consult your dictionary or other appropriate reference book.) Following each selection, we ask you to "think about" the writer's development of the main idea, the method of organization, and specific uses of language. The "Write about" section provides a writing assignment, and the "Try out" section that follows suggests specific ways you can use some of the writer's techniques in your own writing.

Throughout the text, then, you will find that as you learn to read increasingly complex writings thoughtfully, you will also be developing your ability to write what you want to say in a way that will be understood by the people you want to say it to. And we also believe that as you practice effective writing, you will be readying yourself to read a wide range of material with understanding, with ease, and with enjoyment.

H. P. T. and S. F. T.

- **Expression of Feeling**
- **Description**

# EXPRESSION OF FEELING

*Selection One*

---

*Tennis Power*

## Look for:

1.  the phrase in the third sentence, "his name, which I forgot immediately." This phrase will give you a clue to what will happen later on to make Cosby feel embarrassed.

2.  the attitude of each of the two strangers as they meet in the elevator. If you were one of these people, would you be happy to play a game with the other? Why or why not?

3.  evidence that Cosby misjudged the other man's "tennis power." Why did he? Might you have done the same?

4.  these words:

    **lob (LAHB, rhymes with job)—the word for the tennis technique which caused the writer some trouble. You may be able to tell what this word means by the way it is used here. If not, check your dictionary.** [2]

    **love (LUV)—in the game of tennis, a score of zero** [2]

    **dink (DINK)—in tennis, a shot that barely goes over the net. From the slang word "dinky," meaning little.** [2]

# Tennis Power

### Bill Cosby

One of the most embarrassing moments I've ever had happened
during my second year of tennis playing. A gentleman on the elevator of the Las Vegas Hilton Hotel said hello to me. I had my tennis
clothes on; I was going down to the court. He told me his name,
which I forgot immediately because I thought he was just some guy
on the elevator. He asked me how the courts were and I said the
courts were fine, and he asked me if I was going down to play and
I said yes. He said, "I'd like to come down and play with you." And
I said, "Fine, come down." (I play with anybody because—well—
I just love to play.)

The man looked to be fifty years old. Nice-looking, kinda thin. I
went down, talked with the pro, told him I had a game and booked the
court. All I can remember from the set we played was that this man
returned everything I hit. I realized that he could hit after I warmed
up with him, but I figured there must be some things that he couldn't
hit. But the man was always there, even on my little dink shots that
dropped over the net. He had a wonderful way of surprising me with a
lob. It seemed that no matter where I went, a lob was going over my
head. Now at this particular time, I had not learned an important
thing about the lob. You see, you can better your chances of getting a
ball that's been lobbed over your head if you (1) realize that it is a lob,
(2) do not stand there and watch it. I was just amazed at the lob and
just wanted to stand there to see how high it would go. And then, as it
reached its peak, I would turn around and run after it, which, of
course, worked to my disadvantage. Well, needless to say, the man
won the set, 6–love. I was so tired chasing all those lobs I was glad it
was over. He must have lobbed about seven hundred times; each time
I would chase it down and do some ridiculous thing like running with
my back turned to him, catching the ball as it bounced away from me,

hitting it back over my shoulder with the racket following through, hitting myself in the face. The ball would go back on his court. He would then hit something soft to me (nothing he hit was hard). I would hit back some dink way much like a ping-pong player. I would then rush to the net because volleying was my strongest point—so I thought. And then, this lob would show up again and there I was running back again, watching the ball go up in the air and saying to myself things like "That's a lob."

3    So when I finished this 6–love set, it was three o'clock in the afternoon. People had gathered around and I thought it was their interest in Bill Cosby. Later I learned that I had been making a fool of myself with Frank Parker, who for many years ranked in the top ten of the U.S. Lawn Association and won Forest Hills in 1944. I'm happy to say that Frank Parker and I teamed up in July 1974 and won the Pro Celebrity Tennis Match in Chicago. We beat Tony Trabert and Charlton Heston, but I can never forget the day Frank beat me, 6–love.

## Think about:

1.    why the phrase "making a fool of myself" in the last paragraph sums up the main idea that Cosby has been implying all along. Can you give some reasons why Cosby feels this way about the whole incident?

2.    how this selection reminds you of the way Cosby sounds on television. What phrases do you find here that sound like Cosby's speaking style?

## Write about:

one of the most _____ moments in your life. The word you choose may be *embarrassing* or *exciting* or *boring* or *peaceful* or something else. Describe the experience showing exactly what happened that caused you to feel the way you do about the incident.

# Try out:

beginning with a direct statement of your main idea, as Cosby does. Use your key word (such as *exciting* or *boring*) in your first sentence. This kind of beginning will probably help you to continue saying what you want to say.

---

*Selection Two*

*Incident*

# Look for:

1.   the narrator's feelings as he tells about the "incident" step by step.

2.   these words:
     **glee (GLEE)—excited happiness, joy, pleasure** [2]
     **Baltimorean (ball-t'-MORE-ee-an)—person whose home is in Baltimore, Maryland** [3]
     **whit (WHIT)—little bit, an indefinite measure but the smallest amount possible** [6]

# Incident

### Countee Cullen

Once riding in old Baltimore,
Heart-filled, head-filled with glee,
I saw a Baltimorean
Keep looking straight at me.

5      Now I was eight and very small,
And he was no whit bigger,
And so I smiled, but he poked out
His tongue, and called me, "Nigger."

I saw the whole of Baltimore
10    From May until December;
Of all the things that happened there
That's all that I remember.

## Think about:

1.    the way the narrator feels at the beginning of the poem (stanza 1).

2.    the response of the other person in the poem to the narrator's friendly gesture (stanza 2).

3.    the narrator's feelings about the "incident"—at the time it happened and apparently forever afterward (stanza 3).

"Incident" from *On These I Stand* by Countee Cullen. Copyright 1925 by Harper & Row, Publishers, Inc.; renewed 1953 by Ida M. Cullen. Reprinted by permission of Harper & Row, Publishers, Inc.

## Write about:

an incident involving yourself in which you were deeply affected—for good or ill—by another person's words or actions. The experience need not be like the poet's. Perhaps you remember a time when someone you didn't know very well was especially kind to you—or a time when a teacher misunderstood you, making you feel bad in front of your class.

## Try out:

first, grabbing a pen or pencil and writing as fast as you can all that you remember about the incident. Just write down everything that comes to your mind about what happened and how you felt about it.

then rewriting, this time paying more attention to making your thoughts clear to a reader. To accomplish this, try following the order that Cullen follows. That is, try telling first how you felt before the incident, next what some other person did or said, and then how you felt as a result of this encounter.

*On Being 17, Bright, and Unable to Read*

# Look for:

1.   the incident that David Raymond, a high-school student, uses in this newspaper article to start the reader thinking about his problem.

2.   Raymond's feelings about his handicap. Note that he tells directly in several places how he felt in various situations.

3.   these words:
     **psychiatrist (s'-KI-uh-trist)—a doctor, with an M.D. degree, who treats mental and emotional problems** [6]

     **dyslexia (diss-LEX-ee-ah)—inability to read, probably because of problems in the physical nervous system** [7]

# On Being 17, Bright, and Unable to Read

David Raymond

One day a substitute teacher picked me to read aloud from the 1
textbook. When I told her "No, thank you," she came unhinged.
She thought I was acting smart, and told me so. I kept calm, and
that got her madder and madder. We must have spent 10 minutes
trying to solve the problem, and finally she got so red in the face I
thought she'd blow up. She told me she'd see me after class.

Maybe someone like me was a new thing for that teacher. But she 2
wasn't new to me. I've been through scenes like that all my life. You
see, even though I'm 17 and a junior in high school, I can't read
because I have dyslexia. I'm told I read "at a fourth-grade level," but
from where I sit, that's not reading. You can't know what that means
unless you've been there. It's not easy to tell how it feels when you
can't read your homework assignments or the newspaper or a menu
in a restaurant or even notes from your own friends.

My family began to suspect I was having problems almost from 3
the first day I started school. My father says my early years in school
were the worst years of his life. They weren't so good for me, either.
As I look back on it now, I can't find the words to express how bad
it really was. I wanted to die. I'd come home from school screaming,
"I'm dumb. I'm dumb—I wish I were dead!"

I guess I couldn't read anything at all then—not even my own 4
name—and they tell me I didn't talk as good as other kids. But what
I remember about those days is that I couldn't throw a ball where
it was supposed to go, I couldn't learn to swim, and I wouldn't learn
to ride a bike, because no matter what anyone told me, I knew I'd
fail.

Sometimes my teachers would try to be encouraging. When I 5
couldn't read the words on the board they'd say, "Come on, David,

you know that word." Only I didn't. And it was embarrassing. I just felt dumb. And dumb was how the kids treated me. They'd make fun of me every chance they got, asking me to spell "cat" or something like that. Even if I knew how to spell it, I wouldn't; they'd only give me another word. Anyway, it was awful, because more than anything I wanted friends. On my birthday when I blew out the candles I didn't wish I could learn to read; what I wished for was that the kids would like me.

6    With the bad reports coming from school, and with me moaning about wanting to die and how everybody hated me, my parents began looking for help. That's when the testing started. The school tested me, the child-guidance center tested me, private psychiatrists tested me. Everybody knew something was wrong—especially me.

7    It didn't help much when they stuck a fancy name onto it. I couldn't pronounce it then—I was only in second grade—and I was ashamed to talk about it. Now it rolls off my tongue, because I've been living with it for a lot of years—dyslexia.

8    All through elementary school it wasn't easy. I was always having to do things that were "different," things the other kids didn't have to do. I had to go to a child psychiatrist, for instance.

9    One summer my family forced me to go to a camp for children with reading problems. I hated the idea, but the camp turned out pretty good, and I had a good time. I met a lot of kids who couldn't read and somehow that helped. The director of the camp said I had a higher I.Q. than 90 percent of the population. I didn't believe him.

10    About the worst thing I had to do in fifth and sixth grade was go to a special education class in another school in our town. A bus picked me up, and I didn't like that at all. The bus also picked up emotionally disturbed kids and retarded kids. It was like going to a school for the retarded. I always worried that someone I knew would see me on that bus. It was a relief to go to the regular junior high school.

11    Life began to change a little for me then, because I began to feel better about myself. I found the teachers cared; they had meetings about me and I worked harder for them for a while. I began to work on the potter's wheel, making vases and pots that the teachers said were pretty good. Also, I got a letter for being on the track team. I could always run pretty fast.

At high school the teachers are good and everyone is trying to help 12
me. I've gotten honors some marking periods and I've won a letter
on the cross-country team. Next quarter I think the school might
hold a show of my pottery. I've got some friends. But there are still
some embarrassing times. For instance, every time there is writing
in the class, I get up and go to the special education room. Kids ask
me where I go all the time. Sometimes I say, "to Mars."

Homework is a real problem. During free periods in school I go 13
into the special ed room and staff members read assignments to me.
When I get home my mother reads to me. Sometimes she reads an
assignment into a tape recorder, and then I go into my room and
listen to it. If we have a novel or something like that to read, she
reads it out loud to me. Then I sit down with her and we do the
assignment. She'll write, while I talk my answers to her. Lately I've
taken to dictating into a tape recorder, and then someone—my
father, a private tutor or my mother—types up what I've dictated.
Whatever homework I do takes someone else's time, too. That
makes me feel bad.

We had a big meeting in school the other day—eight of us, four 14
from the guidance department, my private tutor, my parents and
me. The subject was me. I said I wanted to go to college, and they
told me about colleges that have facilities and staff to handle people
like me. That's nice to hear.

As for what happens after college, I don't know and I'm worried 15
about that. How can I make a living if I can't read? Who will hire
me? How will I fill out the application form? The only thing that
gives me any courage is the fact that I've learned about well-known
people who couldn't read or had other problems and still made it.
Like Albert Einstein, who didn't talk until he was 4 and flunked
math. Like Leonardo da Vinci, who everyone seems to think had
dyslexia.

I've told this story because maybe some teacher will read it and 16
go easy on a kid in the classroom who has what I've got. Or, maybe
some parent will stop nagging his kid, and stop calling him lazy.
Maybe he's not lazy or dumb. Maybe he just can't read and doesn't
know what's wrong. Maybe he's scared, like I was.

# Think about:

1. the principal reason the writer was so unhappy in elementary school. Where in the article does he show this unhappiness most strikingly?

2. how Raymond's failure to learn to read made him feel about being able to learn other things.

3. the time when the writer first began to get some help that allowed him to feel hopeful.

4. the writer's attitude toward his problem at the end of the article. Does he have hope for a solution? Why or why not?

5. the organization of this selection. You will find that, like other essays in this book, it has three parts: an **introduction,** a **body** or main section, and a **conclusion.**

   The first two paragraphs of this essay can be considered its introduction. The first paragraph illustrates the problem Raymond is writing about. What does the second paragraph do?

   The body extends from ¶ 3 through ¶ 14. To see how the writer has organized this section, have your pencil in hand as you reread the essay and make notes in the margin to keep track of his **chronological arrangement** (that is, his arrangement of events in the order in which they occurred).

   Paragraphs 15 and 16 make up the conclusion of the essay. Concluding paragraphs usually tie together in some way all that the writer has been saying in the body of the essay. Raymond does this by directly stating his purpose. What is it?

## Write about:

a time in your life when you had a problem you found difficult to cope with. Tell exactly how you felt about having this problem. Show through specific examples like the one in Raymond's first paragraph how other people reacted to you because of it, and tell how you or how you and other people worked to solve the problem. Your problem need not be as serious as Raymond's. Perhaps, for example, you finally learned to swim or finally earned enough money to come to college only after a period of self-doubt and struggle.

## Try out:

again, pouring forth your feelings on paper as you write quickly all that you remember of the situation you are describing.

then, rewriting, that is, preparing a final draft to hand in. This time try beginning by describing an incident that will get the reader interested in your problem (as Raymond does in ¶ 1 where he describes the teacher as becoming "unhinged"). From there you can go on to give details about how the problem affected you and to tell what you did to resolve it. If Raymond's organizational pattern (see *Think about,* #5) seems appropriate, try following it.

Holding the Phone

# Look for:

1.    the telephone solicitor's changing attitude toward her job. What incident finally causes her to make a decision about it?

2.    the conversational *tone* of this article. As you read, can you imagine this speaker talking? This interview was recorded and edited by Studs Terkel for his book, *Working.* What words and phrases sound especially like spoken conversation rather than polished writing? How does this way of writing up the interview help the reader to understand how the worker feels?

3.    these words:
        **subsidizing (SUB-s'-dize-ing)—paying someone a grant or allowance of money to help him or her make ends meet. On a larger scale, the government is subsidizing a private corporation when it provides financial aid to prevent bankruptcy.** [3]
        **solicitor (so-LISS-ih-tor)—a person who asks others to buy goods or services or to contribute money or work for a cause** [5]
        **gimmick (GIM-ik—GIM, not Jim or gym)—a device or kind of trick to attract attention** [8]
        **elated (ee-LATE-ed)—thrilled** [18]

# Holding the Phone

**Studs Terkel**

I needed a job. I saw this ad in the paper: Equal Opportunity. 1
Salary plus commission. I called and spoke ever so nicely. The gentleman was pleased with the tone of my voice and I went down for an
interview. My mind raced as I was on the train coming down. I'll
be working on North Michigan Avenue. It's the greatest street. I was
elated. I got the job right away. All we had to do was get orders for
the newspaper.

We didn't have to think what to say. They had it all written out. 2
You have a card. You'd go down the list and call everyone on the
card. You'd have about fifteen cards with the person's names, ad-
dresses, and phone numbers. "This is Mrs. Du Bois. Could I have
a moment of your time? We're wondering if you now subscribe to
any newspapers? If you would *only* for three short months take this
paper, it's for a worthy cause." To help blind children or Crusade
of Mercy. We'd always have one at hand. "After the three-month
period, if you no longer desire to keep it, you can cancel it. But you
will have helped them. They need you." You'd use your last name.
You could alter your name, if you wanted to. You'd almost have to
be an actress on the phone. (Laughs.) I was very excited about it,
until I got the hang of it.

The salary was only $1.60 an hour. You'd have to get about nine 3
or ten orders per day. If you didn't, they'd pay you only $1.60. They
call that subsidizing you. (Laughs.) If you were subsidized more than
once, you were fired.

The commission depended on the territory. If it was middle class, 4
it would be $3.50. If it was ghetto, it would be like $1.50. Because
some people don't pay their bills. A lot of papers don't get delivered

in certain areas. Kids are afraid to deliver. They're robbed. The suburbs was the top territory.

5    A fair area, say, lower middle class, they'd pay you $2.50. To a lot of solicitors' dismay they'd kill some orders at the end of the week. He'd come in and say, "You don't get this $2.50, because they don't want the paper." We don't know if it's true or not. How do we know they canceled? But we don't get the commission.

6    If you didn't get enough orders for the week, a lot of us would work four and five hours overtime. We knew: no orders, no money. (Laughs.) We'd come down even on Saturdays.

7    They had some old pros, but they worked on the suburbs. I worked the ghetto areas. The old-timers really came up with some doozies. They knew how to psyche people. They were very fast talkers. If a person wanted to get off the phone they'd say, "No, they need you. They need your help. It's only for three short months." The person would just have to say, "Okay," and end up taking it.

8    They had another gimmick. If they kept the paper they would get a free gift of a set of steak knives. If they canceled the order, they wouldn't get anything. Everybody wants something free.

9    There was a chief supervisor. He would walk into the office and say, "Okay, you people, let's get some orders! What do you think this is?" He'd come stomping in and holler, "I could pay all the bums on Madison Street to come in, you know." He was always harassing you. He was a bully, a gorilla of a man. I didn't like the way he treated women.

10    I did as well as I wanted to. But after a while, I didn't care. Surely I could have fast-talked people. Just to continually lie to them. But it just wasn't in me. The disgust was growing in me every minute. I would pray and pray to hold on a little longer. I really needed the money. It was getting more and more difficult for me to make these calls.

11    The supervisor would sometimes listen in. He had connections with all the phones. He could just click you in. If a new girl would come in, he'd have her listen to see how you were doing—to see how well this person was lying. That's what they taught you. After a while, when I got down to work, I wanted to cry.

12    I talked to one girl about it. She felt the same way. But she needed the job too. The atmosphere was different here than being in a

factory. Everybody wants to work on North Michigan Avenue. All the people I've worked with, most of them aren't there any more. They change. Some quit, some were dismissed. The bully would say they weren't getting enough orders. They get the best liar and the best liar stays. I observed, the older people seemed to enjoy it. You could just hear them bugging the people . . .

We'd use one charity and would change it every so often. Different papers have different ones they use. I know a girl does the same work for another paper. The phone room is in the same building as the newspaper. But our checks are paid by the Reader's Service Agency. 13

When I first started I had a pretty good area. They do this just to get you conditioned. (Laughs.) This is easy. I'm talking to nice people. God, some of the others! A few obscenities. A lot of males would say things to you that weren't so pleasant. Some were lonely. They'd tell you that. Their wives had left them . . . 14

At first I liked the idea of talking to people. But pretty soon, knowing the area I was calling—they couldn't afford to eat, let alone buy a newspaper—my job was getting me down. They'd say, "Lady, I have nine to feed or I would help you." What can you say? One woman I had called early in the morning, she had just gotten out of the hospital. She had to get up and answer the phone. 15

They would tell me their problems. Some of them couldn't read, honest to God. They weren't educated enough to read a newspaper. Know what I would say? "If you don't read anything but the comic strips . . ." "If you got kids, they have to learn how to read the paper." I'm so ashamed thinking of it. 16

In the middle-class area, the people were busy and they couldn't talk. But in the poor area, the people really wanted to help the charity I talked about. They said I sounded so nice, they would take it anyway. A lot of them were so happy that someone actually called. They could talk all day long to me. They told me all their problems and I'd listen. 17

They were so *elated* to hear someone nice, someone just to listen a few minutes to something that had happened to them. Somehow to show concern about them. I didn't care if there was no order. So I'd listen. I heard a lot of their life histories on the phone. I didn't care if the supervisor was clicked in. 18

19     People that were there a long time knew just what to do. They knew when to click 'em off and get right on to the next thing. They were just striving, striving . . . It was on my mind when I went home. Oh my God, yeah. I knew I couldn't continue doing it much longer.

20     What really did it for me was one call I made. I went through the routine. The guy listened patiently and he said, "I really would like to help." He was blind himself! That really got me—the tone of his voice. I could just tell he was a good person. He was willing to help even if he couldn't read the paper. He was poor, I'm sure of that. It was the worst ghetto area. I apologized and thanked him. That's when I left for the ladies' room. I was nauseous. Here I was sitting here telling him a bunch of lies and he was poor and blind and willing to help. Taking his money.

21     I got sick in the stomach. I prayed a lot as I stayed there in the restroom. I said, "Dear God, there must be something better for me. I never harmed anyone in my life, dear Lord." I went back to the phone room and I just sat there. I didn't make any calls. The supervisor called me out and wanted to know why I was sitting there. I told him I wasn't feeling good, and I went home.

22     I came back the next day because I didn't have any other means of employment. I just kept praying and hoping and looking. And then, as if my prayers were answered, I got another job. The one I have now. I love it.

23     I walked into the bully's office and told him a few things. I told him I was sick and tired of him. Oh God, I really can't tell you what I said. (Laughs.) I told him, "I'm not gonna stay here and lie for you. You can take your job and shove it." (Laughs.) And I walked out. He just stood there. He didn't say anything. He was surprised. I was very calm, I didn't shout. Oh, I felt good.

24     I still work in the same building. I pass him in the hallway every once in a while. He never speaks to me. He looks away. Every time I see him I hold my head very high, very erect, and keep walking.

## Think about:

1.  details Terkel provides about Du Bois' working conditions. What does she dislike most about this job? If you had this job, would you feel the same way about it?

2.  why Enid Du Bois laughs on several occasions and why Terkel makes a note of this laughter.

3.  other ways the writer could have given the information in this article. For instance, he could have taken all his questions and all her answers from the tape recorder and had them printed. Or he could have written an essay about what she told him without quoting her at all. In what ways does the method he chose help you understand how the worker feels about her job? Why do you suppose Terkel chose the method he did?

## Write about:

your feelings about a job you have held that you especially liked or disliked. If you disliked it, tell what you had to do or were not allowed to do on that job. If you liked the job, tell what you had a chance to do that you wanted to do and considered worth doing.

## Try out:

using language you would use in talking to a friend about this job as you express enthusiasm, complaints, "the blahs," or whatever you really feel.

again, letting your first draft come very freely. Then, as you write your draft to hand in, organize your thoughts as you would if you were telling a friend about how the job got better or worse as time went on. In this second draft you can "edit out" any language you feel is not appropriate.

quoting directly one or more of the people you are writing about—your boss, fellow workers, or yourself—if this technique fits what you want to say. Note how Terkel uses this technique in ¶ 9, where Enid Du Bois quotes her boss as saying, "Okay, you people, let's get some orders! . . ." Note also that the writer uses quotation marks just before the person begins speaking and again at the end of the speaker's words. If you quote two or more people speaking to each other—that is, if you use **dialogue**—be sure to set off each speaker's remarks by quotation marks at the beginning and end.

# DESCRIPTION

Selection Five

*The House*

## Look for:

1. the very specific description of the design and structure of the house.

2. these words:
    **chambers (CHAME-berz)—rooms** [1]
    **commodious (cum-MODE-ee-us)—large, roomy, spacious** [5]
    **awry (uh-RYE)—off center, pushed or fallen from a balanced position, twisted aside** [7]

# The House

**James Agee**

1    Two blocks, of two rooms each, one room behind another. Between these blocks a hallway, floored and roofed, wide open both at front and rear: so that these blocks are two rectangular yoked boats, or floated tanks, or coffins, each, by an inner wall, divided into two squared chambers. The roof, pitched rather steeply from front and rear, its cards met and nailed at a sharp angle. The floor faces the earth closely. On the left of the hall, two rooms, each an exact square. On the right a square front room and, built later, behind it, using the outward weatherboards for its own front wall, a leanto kitchen half that size.

2    At the exact center of each of the outward walls of each room, a window. Those of the kitchen are small, taller than wide, and are glassed. Those of the other rooms are exactly square and are stopped with wooden shutters.

3    From each room a door gives on the hallway. The doors of the two front rooms are exactly opposite: the doors of the rear rooms are exactly opposite. The two rooms on either side of the hallway are also connected inwardly by doors through their partition walls.

4    Out at the left of the house, starting from just above the side window of the front room, a little roof is reached out and rested on thin poles above bare ground: shelter for wagon or for car.

5    At the right of the house, just beneath the side window of the front room, a commodious toolbox, built against the wall. It is nailed shut.

6    The hallway yields onto a front porch about five feet long by ten wide, reaching just a little short of the windows at either side, set at dead center of the front of the house. A little tongue of shingles, the same size, is stuck out slightly slanted above it,

From *Let Us Now Praise Famous Men* by James Agee. Copyright © renewed 1969 by Mia Fritsch Agee. Reprinted by permission of Houghton Mifflin Company.

and is sustained on four slender posts from which most of the bark has been stripped.

Three steps lead down at center; they are of oak: the bottom one is cracked and weak, for all its thickness. Stones have been stacked beneath it, but they have slid awry, and it goes to the ground sharply underfoot. Just below and beyond it is a wide flat piece of shale the color of a bruise. It is broken several ways across and is sunken into the dirt.

## Think about:

1.  the writer's use of **factual language**—language that refers to objects or happenings that could be proven to exist or occur. Do you find any words or phrases that refer to feelings, impressions, or attitudes—words like "good" or "bad," "beautiful" or "ugly," "tumbledown shack" or "snug cottage"? Words like these are sometimes called **judgment words.**

2.  the picture this piece of writing creates. Try to see in your mind just what this house looks like. Reading Agee's purposefully factual language, you can decide for yourself what you think about how the house looks—good, bad, mediocre? ugly, plain, good-looking? well-planned, reasonably put together, a disorganized mess?

3.  Agee's use of sentence fragments—groups of words that do not make complete statements—throughout this selection. Why do you think he uses this unconventional style in his descriptions here? Writing sentence fragments is not a useful technique unless a writer has a clear idea of what he or she wants to accomplish by using them. What does Agee emphasize here by leaving out verbs in most of his "sentences"? In your own writing, avoiding sentence fragments is usually a good idea because their use often appears to be the result of careless writing habits.

## Write about:

a structure or large manufactured object that you have seen and known. This object could be a house or other building, a car or other vehicle, a bridge or pier or a traffic interchange, or even a large piece of furniture such as an old-fashioned roll-top desk. Describe this object by telling how it is constructed.

## Try out:

working toward a final draft that uses *factual language* all the way through, as Agee's does. In order to be sure of your facts, first go back to the place or object you intend to write about and check such things as shapes, measurements, and details of structure that you have previously observed. Take notes on all these things, and write your first draft as soon as possible afterward. It will be a good idea to jot down the first draft just as it comes to you, as you have been doing for previous assignments. But if you are like most people, in your first draft you will probably include some words or phrases that express your feelings about this object or structure, especially if it is something that is familiar to you. Therefore, you should go back over this first draft and edit —that is, cut out or change—any words or phrases that seem to judge rather than simply report facts that can be measured or proved.

You probably found that Agee's description includes no *judgment words* (or almost none—"commodious" might be an exception). When he describes (¶ 4) the extension to the left of the house (a sort of carport), he simply tells exactly how it looked and how it was built; he does not say, for instance, whether he considers it ugly or attractive, adequate or inadequate. And when he describes the windows, he does not tell how well he likes them; he tells only their size, shape, and placement. Agee's wording here can serve as a good model for you in this assignment of writing factual description. Later, you will have a chance to read and write description that combines fact and feeling.

*The Hamburger Stand*

# Look for:

1.  the picture the writer creates of a short-order restaurant of the type that was common on cross-country highways in the 1930s. What kinds of places serve the same purpose today?

2.  the writer's use of factual language. Does Steinbeck give more than "the bare facts"?

3.  these words:
    **irritated (EAR-ih-tate-ed)—annoyed, somewhat angry**
    [5]

    **custom (CUSS-tum)—business, especially repeat business** [5]

    **bridles (BRIDE-'lz)—pulls back and tenses up** [5]

    **vivaciousness (viv-A-shuss-ness)—liveliness, a happy, playful, enthusiastic manner** [5]

    **spatula (SPAT-choo-la)—a flat, wide utensil used in cooking to lift and turn pancakes, hamburgers, etc.**
    [5]

    **quoit (KWOYT)—a ring of stiff material used in a game called "quoits," which is much like "horseshoes" or "ring-toss." You try to toss the quoit over a metal spike.** [5]

# The Hamburger Stand

**John Steinbeck**

1    Along 66 the hamburger stands—Al & Susy's Place—Carl's Lunch—Joe & Minnie—Will's Eats. Board-and-bat shacks. Two gasoline pumps in front, a screen door, a long bar, stools, and a foot rail. Near the door three slot machines, showing through glass the wealth in nickels three bars will bring. And beside them, the nickel phonograph with records piled up like pies, ready to swing out to the turntable and play dance music, "Ti-pi-ti-pi-tin," "Thanks for the Memory," Bing Crosby, Benny Goodman. At one end of the counter a covered case; candy cough drops, caffeine sulphate called Sleepless, No-Doze; candy, cigarettes, razor blades, aspirin, Bromo-Seltzer, Alka-Seltzer. The walls decorated with posters, bathing girls, blondes with big breasts and slender hips and waxen faces, in white bathing suits, and holding a bottle of Coca-Cola and smiling—see what you get with a Coca-Cola. Long bar, and salts, peppers, mustard pots, and paper napkins. Beer taps behind the counter, and in back the coffee urns, shiny and steaming, with glass gauges showing the coffee level. And pies in wire cages and oranges in pyramids of four. And little piles of Post Toasties, corn flakes, stacked up in designs.

2    The signs on cards, picked out with shining mica: Pies Like Mother Used to Make. Credit Makes Enemies, Let's Be Friends. Ladies May Smoke But Be Careful Where You Lay Your Butts. Eat Here and Keep Your Wife for a Pet. IITYWYBAD?

3    Down at one end the cooking plates, pots of stew, potatoes, pot roast, roast beef, gray roast pork waiting to be sliced.

4    Minnie or Susy or Mae, middle-aging behind the counter, hair curled and rouge and powder on a sweating face. Taking orders in a soft low voice, calling them to the cook with a screech like a

peacock. Mopping the counter with circular strokes, polishing the big shining coffee urns. The cook is Joe or Carl or Al, hot in a white coat and apron, beady sweat on white forehead, below the white cook's cap; moody, rarely speaking, looking up for a moment at each new entry. Wiping the griddle, slapping down the hamburger. He repeats Mae's orders gently, scrapes the griddle, wipes it down with burlap. Moody and silent.

Mae is the contact, smiling, irritated, near to outbreak; smiling while her eyes look on past—unless for truck drivers. There's the backbone of the joint. Where the trucks stop, that's where the customers come. Can't fool truck drivers, they know. They bring the custom. They know. Give 'em a stale cup a coffee an' they're off the joint. Treat 'em right an' they come back. Mae really smiles with all her might at truck drivers. She bridles a little, fixes her back hair so that her breasts will lift with her raised arms, passes the time of day and indicates great things, great times, great jokes. Al never speaks. He is no contact. Sometimes he smiles a little at a joke, but he never laughs. Sometimes he looks up at the vivaciousness in Mae's voice, and then he scrapes the griddle with a spatula, scrapes the grease into an iron trough around the plate. He presses down a hissing hamburger with his spatula. He lays the split buns on the plate to toast and heat. He gathers up stray onions from the plate and heaps them on the meat and presses them in with the spatula. He puts half the bun on top of the meat, paints the other half with melted butter, with thin pickle relish. Holding the bun on the meat, he slips the spatula under the thin pad of meat, flips it over, lays the buttered half on top, and drops the hamburger on a small plate. Quarter of a dill pickle, two black olives beside the sandwich. Al skims the plate down the counter like a quoit. And he scrapes his griddle with the spatula and looks moodily at the stew kettle.

# Think about:

1.	the purpose of the writer's use of factual language. Note that this selection is from a work of **fiction.** Steinbeck is writing about objects and happenings that *could* exist and occur, although he doubtless did not experience this whole scene exactly as he relates it here. He is using factual language in order to create not only a picture of a fictional "hamburger stand" but also to create a feeling or impression about the place and the people found there. What is this feeling or impression? That is, if you were a truck driver, would you consider it an adequate place to stop for lunch? Or if you were a waitress or fry cook, would you consider working there to be an acceptable job? Why or why not?

2.	the way the author's factual language includes **specific details** to make the kind of place he is describing seem real to the reader. For example, note the group of words beginning with "The walls decorated with posters . . ." If he had stopped there, using only the **general term** "poster," what kind of poster would you imagine? (What would you "see" in your mind? A big blank sheet of cardboard? Your own favorite rock star poster? Palm trees in a travel ad?) But Steinbeck does not stop there. He adds details to show the reader what the posters in "hamburger stands" look like. Find other examples of Steinbeck's use of a general descriptive term (a word like "poster") followed by details that make clear exactly how the object or person looked or acted.

3.	the selection of details that the writer makes to describe the people he wants us to visualize. What specific details does he mention about Mae the waitress and Al the fry cook that show how they fit the scene? Why does he not tell more about them as individuals—their appearance, their personal lives and interests?

4.	Steinbeck's use of sentence fragments. Note that, like Agee, Steinbeck uses fragments for emphasis. What is he emphasizing here by using fragments?

## Write about:

a familiar public place, describing it in exact detail. The place might be a bus station, your school cafeteria, an auto repair shop or gas station, a sports arena after a game, the local post office. Tell specifically what furniture or equipment is there and how it is being used, what people are there and exactly what they are doing. Mention shapes, colors, sounds, and smells—in short, anything that will show your readers exactly what the place is like.

## Try out:

visiting the place, shortly before writing about it. Observe carefully exactly what is there, what is happening, and who is doing what. Take notes, using very detailed language. If you observe wheels, for example, how big are they? What color? Are they of a special type or for a special purpose? Then, when you write, put down the details that will be most likely to make the scene clear to the reader.

*Squirrel Near Library*

# Look for:

1.  exact words and phrases with which the writer describes the squirrel.

2.  the challenge in line 3. Are there days when you feel as "alive" as a squirrel?

3.  these words:
    **Disney (DIZ-nee)—refers to Walt Disney, creator of Mickey Mouse and various other fictional animals. The poet uses the word "Disney" here as an adjective; she implies that the squirrel's outline looks like that of a squirrel picture in a Disney film.** [4]

    **silhouette (sill-oo-ET)—outline of a person, animal, or object totally filled in with one color, usually black.** [4]

    **intensively (in-TEN-siv-lee)—very actively, with extreme concentration** [7]

    **tamp (TAMP)—to pat or push down neatly in place (pipe smokers usually *tamp* down tobacco in their pipes before smoking)** [16]

# Squirrel Near Library

### Genevieve Taggard

All he owns is
His body and a few nuts.
He is 300 times as alive as you.
Disney silhouette on a branch,
Headlong creeping, tail afloat, then up, up,       5
And he sits,
Intensively busy, frisking
Tail, plump tum and small
Able paws. Watch, it's run, ripple, stop,
Stop, run and ripple,       10
A thousand times a day.
Tired never. Idle never. But always
Squirrel-alert in a close fitting
Comfortable allover fur suit.
All the shut dictionaries reading RODENT       15
Can't tamp down that
Tail.

## Think about:

1.    the way the poem seems to follow the squirrel on its daily activities. Does the poem help you remember a squirrel—or some other animal—you have observed?

2.    particular words that suggest the idea of the squirrel's quickness and energy.

"Squirrel Near Library" from *Long View* by Genevieve Taggard. Copyright 1938, 1939, 1940, 1941, 1942 by Genevieve Taggard. Renewed in the name of Kenneth Durant 1968, 1969, 1970. Reprinted by permission of Harper & Row, Publishers, Inc.

3.     the poet's attitude toward the dictionary definition. Why is it that definitions are often unsatisfactory—especially those of living creatures?

## Write about:

a creature you observe—a lizard, a cat, a spider, a mouse, or whatever—that you consider interesting for its way of moving. Describe the movement of one individual animal as you see it in motion.

## Try out:

carefully observing the creature for a few minutes before you write. Take some notes, using language that describes particular movements of particular parts of the body. Does the creature jump or jerk? Does it slide or glide? How, exactly, does it move its head, legs, stomach muscles, tail, or whatever body parts it must use to get where it's going or to do what it's doing?

When you begin writing, make the first sentence a direct statement of your main idea (as you did in the assignment for "Tennis Power," page 6). You will probably be writing a single paragraph. Therefore, this opening sentence will be a **topic sentence**—a general statement of the idea of the paragraph. Although topic sentences do not always appear at the beginnings of paragraphs, the technique of starting a paragraph with a topic sentence and then following with specific details is one that successful writers frequently use. It is one which you will be asked to use in many of the writing assignments in this book.

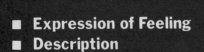
- **Expression of Feeling**
- **Description**
- **Narration**
- **Exposition**

# LEVEL
# TWO

# EXPRESSION
# OF FEELING

*Sorrow Home*

## Look for:

1.    the reason for the sorrow that Margaret Walker first mentions in the title.

2.    specific details that tell where the narrator's home was.

3.    clues about the approximate period in history in which this poem was written. For instance, do you suppose Walker wrote it before or after the Civil Rights movement?

4.    these words:
      **weaned (WEEND)—taken away from mother's milk** [2]
      **sired (SYRD)—fathered. (A sire is the male parent, whether human or any other mammal.)** [2]
      **"L" (EL)—abbreviation for an elevated railroad, often running right alongside apartment windows. Sometimes spelled "el."** [10]
      **fallow (FAL-loh)—unplanted, lying idle during a growing season** [13]

# Sorrow Home

**Margaret Walker**

My roots are deep in southern life; deeper than John Brown
    or Nat Turner or Robert Lee. I was sired and weaned
    in a tropic world. The palm tree and banana leaf,
    mango and cocoanut, breadfruit and rubber trees
    know me.        5

Warm skies and gulf blue streams are in my blood. I belong
    with the smell of fresh pine, with the trail of coon,
    and the spring growth of wild onion.

I am no hot-house bulb to be reared in steam-heated flats
    with the music of "L" and subway in my ears, walled    10
    in by steel and wood and brick far from the sky.

I want the cotton fields, tobacco and the cane. I want to walk
    along with sacks of seed to drop in fallow ground.
    Restless music is in my heart and I am eager to be
    gone.        15

O Southland, sorrow home, melody beating in my bone and
    blood! How long will the Klan of hate, the hounds
    and the chain gangs keep me from my own?

# Think about:

1. details the poet gives that show a contrast between the life she remembers at home and the life she is apparently living at the time she writes the poem.

2. why the narrator wishes she could go back home. Is she likely to go? Why or why not?

3. the strong, specific language used throughout the poem. Look back and find particularly exact nouns and adjectives and verbs that are striking and precise. What especially vivid phrases linger in your mind?

# Write about:

your feelings about a particular place where you have lived or visited—either a place that you like very much and feel at home in or one you would rather not have to stay in. Note that the word "place" is a *general term* that can be used to mean any area from a whole country to a corner of a small room. Be sure you decide on the exact area you want to write about. For example, if you are writing about Louisiana, are you writing about the whole state? Or are you writing only about the farmlands of Louisiana? Or only about the city of New Orleans—or, even more specifically—a particular home there or a small jazz club on Canal Street? Usually, the smaller the area, the easier it is to describe what's there and your feelings about it.

# Try out:

getting across your feelings by using details that describe things and experiences you recall that made this place pleasant or unpleasant for you. Note that the details Walker uses—*palm tree* and *the smell of fresh pine, hounds* and *the chain gangs, steam-heated flats* and *subway*—communicate her feelings to the reader. Through details like these, she shows the reader what she misses at her rural home, why she cannot feel at home there now, and what she dislikes about city living. Often, details like the ones this poet uses communicate feeling better than words that "talk" about feeling. This is especially true when these "talk" words are general terms like "love," "hate," "fear"; "good," "bad," "ugly," "pretty"; interesting," "wonderful," and, above all, "nice." If you use such words in the paper you are writing for this assignment, use them sparingly. As much as possible, show exactly what you have seen and heard that made you love, like, dislike, or hate the place you are writing about.

Begin with a topic sentence that states the main idea your paragraph will develop, as you did in the writing assignment for "Squirrel Near Library." For example, you might want to begin with "Kalamazoo, Michigan, is a _____ city" or "My grandfather's greenhouse was the kind of place I liked when I was a little kid because _____."

Coping With Dad

# Look for:

1. the possible **implications** (or suggested meanings) of the title. (See *these words,* #4 below, for a definition of "coping.") Think of various ways in which different people cope with their parents. Then, as you read this writer's essay, look for the particular ways in which Hayes finds herself coping with her father.

2. the writer's feelings about her father.

3. the time span between the beginning of Hayes' account and the ending of it. How many days go by here? What happens on each of these days?

4. these words:
   **coping (KOHP-ing)—managing, getting along in a diffi-cult situation, overcoming problems, keeping up with an opponent in a contest** [title, 21]

   **wan (WAHN)—pale or ashen as from suffering (either physical or emotional)** [1, 24]

   **erratic (air-RAT-ik)—in a scattered way, off-again-on-again, unpredictable** [3]

   **larynx (LAAR-inks)—voice box, area in upper end of trachea containing the vocal cords** [7]

   **ominously (AHM-uh-nuss-lee)—threateningly, as though warning of doom (from the word "omen")** [22]

# Coping With Dad

**Barbara Hayes**

On a Saturday afternoon in January of 1975, I had come home 1
to visit briefly with my parents before I went to work that evening.
Dad, Mom had told me, had been sober for several days. He hadn't
been feeling well and he never drank when he was sick. When I
walked into the living room that day he was sitting in his leather
chair. His face was wan and repentant. In my lifetime I seldom saw
him sober. He wasn't a quiet alcoholic but rather a loud and vicious
one, and I spent most of my childhood hiding from him, avoiding
him, hating him, and feeling sorry for him. Regardless, though, of
this erratic relationship, out of our family of four I was the only one
who really understood my dad's behavior. I knew why he laughed at
some things and why he became furious at others. Even though his
anger was often unreasonable, I always understood it. And he knew
that I did. When he was sober, as he was on this Saturday, he was
very quiet, smiling with reluctance, and calling little if any attention
to himself.

I stayed at the house for about thirty minutes. Mom always 2
wanted me to stay longer or come more often because she said Dad
missed me, but I always feared he'd be drunk, and I couldn't tolerate
that any longer. Dad was in his room when I was leaving so I went
in there to say goodbye. I hugged him and kissed him on the cheek,
but he didn't respond to me as he usually did. Instead, he almost
turned away as though he were afraid to look at me. As I drove away
I felt the sadness that I always felt when I left my house.

The following Monday evening I received a phone call from 3
Mom. Her voice was quivering and slightly frantic.

"Your father and I went to the City of Hope today and he has 4
pneumonia."

"Coping With Dad" by Barbara Hayes. A previously unpublished work submitted as a
student paper in a class taught by Professor Halsey P. Taylor at California State Polytechnic University, Pomona, California. Reprinted by permission of the author.

5   "Pneumonia? Well, where is he? Is he in the hospital?"

6   "No, he's home. They said he'd be OK at home."

7   "Well then, don't worry, Mom. They wouldn't send him home if they thought there'd be any danger." Dad had had his larynx removed and needed to be very cautious about respiratory illnesses.

8   "I know, but I'm so worried about him. He looks terrible."

9   "Don't worry, Mom. He'll be OK. Did they give him anything to take?"

10  "Yes."

11  "Well then, it's all right. Really, Mom, it's OK." I hoped I had convinced her, but she was terribly upset. She worried constantly about my father. I didn't think much more about it because I knew that in a few days he'd be feeling fine and drinking and raising hell again. My mom would then be wondering why she was so concerned about him.

12  At 7:30 on Tuesday morning the phone rang. My roommate answered and it was for me. I took the receiver.

13  "Hello." It was Mom.

14  "Barbara. Oh Barbara! Come to the hospital!"

15  "What? Hello? What!" There was a long pause. No one was there. Then she returned.

16  "Oh Barbara!"

17  "What, Mom!"

18  "Your father's dead!"

19  "Oh, God, No . . . NO!" I tried to push the words away but they were cold, strong, and stubborn.

20  "Barbara, come to the hospital. No, come home, Barbara. Come home."

21  *Your father's dead.* Those words weren't real. They didn't belong together, in that order. They didn't make sense. They did and then they didn't. The reality flashed in and out. Coping with Dad alive was difficult, but coping with him dead—I couldn't do it.

22  In the hours that followed, relatives and friends were in and out of the house. My brother and his wife flew down from San Francisco. Food came into the house. People were shocked, sorry, comforting, and helpful. Then came the day of the funeral. The long black limousine ominously invited my family and me into its clean wide chambers. It seemed to float down the streets to the funeral home. A soft hand helped me out and led me to the door. I entered

the cool quiet room, hardly believing I was there for Dad's funeral. Then I saw the casket and the sight of it filled up the entire room. My breathing stopped and I reached for something to cling to, but there was nothing except the room, me, and the casket, draped with the red and white stripes of the flag. A wild rush circled through my head as short uncertain steps carried me to that grand box which held my father, and my body trembled as I ran my hands over the stripes and stars. Finally I breathed out, "Oh Daddy," and put my head where I thought his was.

When I stepped back I saw the beautiful flowers, my brother  23
sobbing, and family, friends, and Dad's coworkers humbly entering the room. I took my seat in the first pew and was comforted by the minister's words. I now knew that my father had found peace, as he had suffered so many years of hell. I reflected on years past, on the bad times, the frightening times, and my mind silenced the memories. It replaced those nightmares with pictures of Dad laughing and loving.

For many months after that day, the most painful moments I felt  24
were those when I remembered the pain and loneliness my father knew. And I still think of that Saturday afternoon and my brief visit, his wan face, and how he knew he'd never see me again.

## Think about:

1.   Hayes' use of *connotative* language. Often a writer chooses words—particularly *judgment words* (see p. 24) because of their **connotations**—that is, because the words suggest feelings or thoughts the writer associates with past experiences. Note the *connotations* of the words "coping" (in the title and in ¶21), "wan" (¶1 and ¶ 24), and "grand" (¶ 22) as Hayes uses them in this essay.

"Coping" is a good example of a word that has different

connotations for different people. You have already thought of a number of ways people "cope" or get along with their parents, and each of these ways would represent a different connotation of the word. To one person, "coping" might stand for his or her continual efforts to be agreeable to a parent; to another, "coping" might stand for silence and making oneself scarce. What connotations do you find in the word "coping" as Hayes uses it in this essay? What does she imply when she says, "Coping with Dad alive was difficult, but coping with him dead—I couldn't do it"?

"Wan" can be considered a key word in the essay because it appears in both the first and the last paragraphs. Why do you suppose the author uses this word instead of "pale" or "white-faced" or "sickly"? What *connotations* does "wan" have that these words do not? (Think about the sound of the word as well as its specific meaning.)

"Grand," a word which has several dictionary meanings, also has many different *connotations* for different people. Check your dictionary for the meanings listed for "grand." Which meaning or meanings applies to Hayes' use of the word? Note also that she uses the adjective "grand" with the noun "box" (instead of "casket"). What is the connotation of the two words together in the phrase "grand box"?

There are other *connotative* uses of language in this selection. Find examples that you think are particularly striking. If you also look back at previous selections, especially Margaret Walker's "Sorrow Home" (see p. 38), you will find many other memorable uses of *connotative language*.

2.    the attitude toward her father that the writer develops throughout the essay. Note especially the way she describes his behavior in ¶ 1, her comment there about how she understood his feelings, and the way she concludes the essay. What do you consider her main idea to be?

3.    the writer's inclusion of some details about her mother's and her brother's feelings as well as her own. Note especially the telephone conversation between Barbara and her mother. What is the writer showing about these people's sense of family? How does the picture she gives of their family life help develop her main idea?

# Write about:

how a person you knew well at some time in your life created a special atmosphere that affected you strongly in some way. Show how you felt when you were around this person. Did he or she cause you to feel comfortable? Uncomfortable? Inspired to pursue your goals? Nervous and frustrated at every turn? Show how the person spoke and acted, especially in relation to you. And show how you responded to the person's words and actions.

# Try out:

writing down, just as they come to you, your impressions of this person and your memories of shared experiences and of ways he or she affected you. (You will be doing here what you did in writing the first drafts of assignments in the "Expression of Feeling" section of Level One.)

Then, in your final draft, give the reader a clear idea of how you felt or still feel about the person you are writing about. Select from your first draft appropriate details you have noted about the person's behavior, appearance, facial expressions, or gestures. You can use these details to show how the person's appearance and behavior affected you. Take particular care to choose words that show exactly how you felt or how you feel. That is, choose words that convey the *connotations* you want your readers to understand.

*Water*

# Look for:

1.    what the narrator tells us he loves and looks forward to, and what, in contrast, he dreads and fears.

2.    the feeling the poet puts across to the reader about "the way it is" in time of drouth, in time of rain.

3.    these words:
       **drouth (DROWTH. This word is also spelled "drought" and in that case pronounced DROWT.)—dry weather, a time of no rainfall** [1]
       **cistern (SIS-tern)—a holding tank for water, especially rainwater; a kind of rain barrel** [13]

# Water

**Wendell Berry**

I was born in a drouth year. That summer
my mother waited in the house, enclosed
in the sun and the dry ceaseless wind,
for the men to come back in the evenings,
bringing water from a distant spring.                              5
Veins of leaves ran dry, roots shrank.
And all my life I have dreaded the return
of that year, sure that it still is
somewhere, like a dead enemy's soul. Fear
of dust in my mouth is always with me,                            10
and I am the faithful husband of the rain,
I love the water of wells and springs
and the taste of roofs in the water of cisterns.
I am a dry man whose thirst is praise
of clouds, and whose mind is something of a cup.                  15
My sweetness is to wake in the night
after days of dry heat, hearing the rain.

## Think about:

1.  phrases in the poem that describe in factual language ex-
    actly what happens or happened—for example, "my mother
    waited in the house."

2.  phrases in the poem that are *metaphorical*. A **metaphor** is
    an expression that suggests a comparison of one thing to

another. For example, in line 15, the idea that the mind is ready to receive learning is expressed by comparing the mind to a cup. What is Wendell Berry's metaphor for his continuing love of rainfall?

3.      why he compares the "drouth year" of his birth to a "dead enemy's soul." What is he really afraid of? Technically, "like a dead enemy's soul" is a *simile* (SIM-ill-ee). A **simile,** a kind of metaphorical expression, uses the word *like* or the word *as* to make a direct comparison. What other similes—perhaps expressions that people use all the time—can you think of offhand?

## Write about:

a feeling you have for or against some element of your environment. Are you especially happy when you are by the ocean or a river? Out in the desert? Up in the mountains? In the midst of activity in the city? Is there something about your favorite environment that makes you feel good—that maybe even seems to you to promise a good life, fulfillment, happiness? Analyze what it is about this environment that makes you feel good: it might be the comfortableness of the setting or the stimulation of activities going on around you. Or it might be just the quality of the air, whether damp and foggy or crisp and dry or full of familiar smells. Or perhaps you want to share your feelings about something uncomfortable in an environment. For example, maybe you feel strongly about unpleasant smells that distract you or loud, sudden noises that interrupt you in the midst of your home life in the city. Or you may find intolerable the constantly blowing wind that stirs up sand and dust in the desert.

Note that this project is very similar to the writing assignment you did for "Sorrow Home." The principal difference is that this time you will be writing about a more *general* topic than you chose for "Sorrow Home" (even if you selected a large place like a state or city for that assignment). You will not be writing about a particular place but about a *kind of place or environment.* For example, if you choose to write about city life, you will write about experiences common to people in most cities; you will not describe experiences that happen only in Portland, Oregon, or only in midtown Manhattan in New York City.

## Try out:

in the paragraph you write for this assignment, using "for example" and "for instance" to show what makes you feel the way you do about this kind of place or environment. Again, your first sentence will be your topic sentence. If you want to, you can start with a simple statement such as "I like being in the city because so many exciting things are happening there." Then you can follow with **examples** of the kind of activity you enjoy doing or watching to support your topic sentence.

In addition, try to come up with at least one *metaphor* of your own to show the reader what the activity or atmosphere you are writing about (or some detail of it) reminds you of.

# DESCRIPTION

*The Old Sea-Dog*

## Look for:

1.  the way the first sentence of this paragraph from *Treasure Island* serves as a topic sentence. That is, note that this sentence introduces the main idea, which the rest of the paragraph develops.

2.  details of the "old sea-dog's" behavior that show in what ways and why he was "a very silent man." What did he do in particular that caused the boy who tells the story to notice and remember him?

3.  these words:

    **parlour (PAR-ler)—a living room, especially one in large old homes, that is reserved for special guests or occasions (in the United States, spelled "parlor")**
    [1]

    **desirous (dee-ZIRE-us)—full of desire or longing** [1]

# The Old Sea-Dog

**Robert Louis Stevenson**

He was a very silent man by custom. All day he hung round the     1
cove, or upon the cliffs, with a brass telescope; all evening he sat in
a corner of the parlour next the fire, and drank rum and water very
strong. Mostly he would not speak when spoken to; only look up
sudden and fierce, and blow through his nose like a fog-horn; and
we and the people who came about our house soon learned to let him
be. Every day, when he came back from his stroll, he would ask if
any seafaring men had gone by along the road? At first we thought
it was the want of company of his own kind that made him ask this
question; but at last we began to see he was desirous to avoid them.
When a seaman put up at the "Admiral Benbow" (as now and then
some did, making by the coast road for Bristol), he would look in at
him through the curtained door before he entered the parlour; and
he was always sure to be as silent as a mouse when any such was
present. For me, at least, there was no secret about the matter; for
I was, in a way, a sharer in his alarms. He had taken me aside one
day, and promised me a silver fourpenny on the first of every month
if I would only keep my "weather-eye open for a seafaring man with
one leg," and let him know the moment he appeared. Often enough,
when the first of the month came round, and I applied to him for
my wage, he would only blow through his nose at me, and stare me
down; but before the week was out he was sure to think better of
it, bring me my fourpenny piece, and repeat his orders to look out
for "the seafaring man with one leg."

From *Treasure Island* by Robert Louis Stevenson, 1883.

# Think about:

1.    how the boy feels about the old sea-dog. Why does he agree to keep his "weather eye" out for the man with one leg?

2.    the mystery and suspense that Stevenson builds throughout this paragraph. What details and repetitions cause you to suspect that something exciting is going to happen?

# Write about:

the behavior of a person you have observed closely. Tell what kind of person this is by letting the reader see how the person acts, talks, moves, or relates to other people. Focus on one particular trait or characteristic, as Stevenson does in "The Old Sea-Dog."

# Try out:

again developing a topic sentence in which you make a general comment. This time, the comment will be about a person's behavior. Then develop this idea by means of examples.

Your topic sentence might be, "My friend Sally moves more rapidly than anyone else I have ever known." Or it could be something like, "My grandmother struck most people as being stiff and dignified, but with young people she knew well she was often relaxed and even silly." Or, "The famous ballplayer, _____ _____, who used to live next door to my cousin, impressed me as a very generous kind of person." If you were going to develop one of these topic sentences, you would proceed by giving examples of incidents or happenings that illustrate the way the man, woman, or child usually acted. What, for instance, did Sally do on one particular occasion that demonstrated her rapid movements? Did she decorate the Christmas tree in fifteen minutes? Or how did the grandmother act "silly"? Did she giggle while telling stories about her boyfriends in the long ago? Or what did the ballplayer do on one or more occasions that caused you to consider him generous? Was he always willing to pile his car full of neighbors when he drove to the beach? As you develop your topic sentence, you will think of similar examples of the way the person you are writing about acted.

*Selection Twelve*

*Going West*

## Look for:

1. the specific language that the poet uses to tell the reader exactly what he sees on his train trip from New York to Los Angeles. Note Reznikoff's selection of details.

2. these words:
   **furrows (FUR-ohz)—small ditches left by a plough as it moves through a field** [2]
   **girders (GER-derz)—beams (usually of steel) used in constructing large buildings or bridges** [20]
   **sparse (SPARSS)—thinly spread, not dense or crowded** [24]
   **sage (SAYJ)—a wild plant that grows abundantly in open land throughout the western, especially southwestern, United States. (The leaves of this plant can be used as flavor in cooking.)** [30]

# Going West

**Charles Reznikoff**

The train leaves New York—leaves the tunnel: yesterday's
  snow
in the corners of roofs, in the furrows of ploughed fields,
under the shelter of the naked trees,
on one side of roads and one bank of streams—
5    wherever the morning sun did not reach it;
turbulent streams running in twenty parallel currents;
slopes showing on top a dark band of naked woods.
Bits of coal rain on the roof of the car,
smoke from the engine is blown in front of the window,
10   and on the flat land beside the rails
the snow is blown about.

Next morning, across the lots, blocks of brand-new houses;
old wooden houses with back porches facing the tracks;
the railway yard widens and the ground is evenly lined with
   rails,
15   and we are in Chicago.
The flat fields on either side covered with dried corn-stalks,
broken a little above the ground and flat on the black earth;
ice in the hollows; shaggy horses
trot away from the train; a colt with lifted hoof
20   looks at us; towers of steel girders, in an endless row,
carry wires on three pairs of arms across the fields. A beam
   to guide planes
flashing in the night.

At last only the morning star is shining;
the plain is covered with sparse yellow grass;

a great herd of cattle—red cattle with white faces and legs—
    grazing.
Hills with flat tops; snow in the hollows on the steep sides;
a cement bridge with a bright new railing;
reddish ground; above a ridge of hills
black mountains, sheets of snow on their sides, black moun-
    tains veined with snow.
Low rolling hills covered with sage; neither house nor cattle.    30
    By nightfall it is snowing.

The dark ground is flat to the river—bright with dawn;
beyond rise the mountains, blue and purple;
the blue of the sky becomes purple, in which a star is shining.
The desert is white with snow, the sage heaped with it;    35
the mountains to the north are white. The train turns
south. We are among rocks:
grey rock and red rock; yellow rock and red rock;
cliffs bare of any growth; walls of red rock crumbling;
a mountain covered with boulders, rocks, and stones;    40
and not a living thing
except a large bird
slowly flying.

The ground beside the roadbed is green with bright grass;
the trees along the muddy river are bright with buds;    45
trees in the hollow have budded and are green with leaves.
Palms in the streets of a town.
Purple and white flowers on the desert.
White sand in smooth waves.
A gravel plain like rippling water.    50
Single lights; many lights; lights along highways, lights along
    streets,
and along the streets of Los Angeles.

# Think about:

1. the absence of metaphors in this poem. Why is the exact language appropriate and enough? (See page 48 on *metaphor.*)

2. why this poem may be considered stirring or satisfying by a person who has a strong feeling for his or her country.

# Write about:

what you have observed from a car, a plane, train, or bus window on a trip or ride—even as short a ride as that between your home and school. Report just what was there, leaving out yourself and your feelings about what you saw. Give fact after fact, detail after detail, as Reznikoff does.

# Try out:

arranging the details you include in chronological order, that is, in the order in which you saw or otherwise experienced them. That way, although you will probably be writing one paragraph, you will not need a topic sentence. You will simply be showing the reader what you saw (and perhaps heard and smelled) as you moved from one place to another on your trip.

# NARRATION

*Selection Thirteen*

*"Surgeon" in a Submarine*

## Look for:

1.  the first clue that the "surgeon" in this account is not fully qualified.

2.  the various ways in which the operating staff prepares for the surgery.

3.  the attitude of the whole submarine crew toward the operation.

4.     the attitude of the patient and of the operating staff toward the "surgeon."

5.     these words:

        aft (AFT)—toward the stern (rear) of the ship [1]

        gobs (GAHBZ)—sailors, old-time slang term for seamen (not officers) in the U.S. Navy [10]

        bulkhead (BULK-hed)—wall, upright partition separating compartments [10]

        electrocardiographer (ee-LEK-tro-car-dee-OGG-raa-fer) —a person who operates a machine that records electrical impulses from a patient's heartbeat [14]

        anesthetist (aa-NESS-thuh-tist)—a professional person who prescribes and administers an anesthetic (such as ether) for an operation [22]

        pincers (PIN-serz)—an instrument like a pair of pliers to pinch something closed [28]

        sulfanilamide (sull-fuh-NILL-uh-myd)—the basic drug in sulfa drugs (developed shortly before penicillin), used to prevent or heal infection [29]

        umbilicus (um-BILL-ih-cuss)—navel, "belly button." Think of umbilical cord (connecting a baby with its mother). [39]

        petrolatum (pet-ro-LAY-tum)—an ointment or salve made from petroleum to prevent drying of the skin [53]

        chromic catgut (KRO-mick CAT-gut)—tough thread made of animal intestine (usually sheep, not cat) and used in this instance as surgical thread [58]

# "Surgeon" in a Submarine

George Weller

"They are giving him ether now," was what they said back in the 1
aft torpedo rooms.

"He's gone under, and they're ready to cut him open," the crew 2
whispered, sitting on their pipe bunks cramped between torpedoes.

One man went forward and put his arm quietly around the shoul- 3
der of another man who was handling the bow diving planes.

"Keep her steady, Jake," he said. "They've just made the first cut. 4
They're feeling around for it now."

"They" were a little group of anxious-faced men with their arms 5
thrust into reversed white pajama coats. Gauze bandages hid all their
expressions except the tensity in their eyes.

"It" was an acute appendix inside Dean Rector of Chautauqua, 6
Kansas. The stabbing pains had become unendurable the day before,
which was Rector's first birthday at sea. He was nineteen years old.

The big depth gauge that looks like a factory clock and stands 7
beside the "Christmas tree" of red and green gauges regulating
the flooding chambers showed where they were. They were
below the surface. And above them were enemy waters crossed
and recrossed by whirring propellers of Japanese destroyers and
transports.

The nearest naval surgeon competent to operate on the nineteen- 8
year-old seaman was thousands of miles and many days away. There
was just one way to prevent the appendix from bursting, and that
was for the crew to operate upon their shipmate themselves.

And that's what they did; they operated upon him. It was proba- 9
bly one of the largest operations in numbers of participants that ever
occurred.

" 'Doc' Lipes Commandeers a Submarine Officers' Wardroom" by George Weller, *Chi-cago Daily News,* December 14, 1942. Reprinted with permission from Field Enterprises, Inc. Conclusion from *A Treasury of Great Reporting,* edited by Louis L. Snyder and Richard B. Morris. Simon & Schuster, 1949. Reprinted by permission.

10     "He says he's ready to take his chance," the gobs whispered from bulkhead to bulkhead.

11     "That guy's regular"—the word traveled from bow planes to propeller and back again.

12     They "kept her steady."

13     The chief surgeon was a twenty-three-year-old pharmacist's mate wearing a blue blouse with white-taped collar and squashy white duck cap. His name was Wheeler B. Lipes. He came from Newcastle near Roanoke, Virginia, and had taken the Navy hospital course in San Diego, thereafter serving three years in the naval hospital at Philadelphia, where his wife lives.

14     Lipes' specialty as laboratory technician was in operating a machine that registers heartbeats. He was classified as an electrocardiographer. But he had seen Navy doctors take out one or two appendixes and thought he could do it. Under the sea, he was given his first chance to operate.

15     There was difficulty about the ether. When below the surface the pressure inside a boat is above the atmospheric pressure. More ether is absorbed under pressure. The submariners did not know how long their operation would last.

16     They did not know how long it would take to find the appendix. They did not know whether there would be enough ether to keep the patient under throughout the operation.

17     They didn't want the patient waking up before they were finished.

18     They decided to operate on the table in the officers' wardroom. In the newest and roomiest American submarine the wardroom is approximately the size of a Pullman-car drawing room. It is flanked by bench seats attached to the wall, and a table occupies the whole room—you enter with knees already crooked to sit down. The only way anyone can be upright in the wardrooms is by kneeling.

19     The operating room was just long enough so that the patient's head and feet reached the two ends without hanging over.

20     First they got out a medical book and read up on the appendix, while Rector, his face pale with pain, lay in the narrow bunk. It was probably the most democratic surgical operation ever performed. Everybody from boxplane man to the cook in the galley knew his role.

21     The cook provided the ether mask. It was an inverted tea strainer. They covered it with gauze.

The twenty-three-year-old "surgeon" had, as his staff of fellow  22
"physicians," all men his senior in age and rank. His anesthetist was
Communications Officer Lieutenant Franz Hoskins of Tacoma,
Washington.

Before they carried Rector to the wardroom, the submarine Cap-  23
tain, Lieutenant Commander W. B. Ferrall of Pittsburgh, asked
Lipes as the "surgeon" to have a talk with the patient.

"Look, Dean, I never did anything like this before," Lipes said.  24
"You don't have much chance to pull through, anyhow. What do
you say?"

"I know just how it is, Doc."  25

It was the first time in his life that anybody had called Lipes  26
"Doc." But there was in him, added to the steadiness that goes with
a submariner's profession, a new calmness.

The operating staff adjusted gauze masks while members of the  27
engineroom crew pulled tight their reversed pajama coats over their
extended arms. The tools were laid out. They were far from perfect
or complete for a major operation. The scalpel had no handle.

But submariners are used to "rigging" things. The medicine chest  28
had plenty of hemostats, which are small pincers used for closing
blood vessels. The machinist "rigged" a handle for the scalpel from
a hemostat.

When you are going to have an operation, you must have some  29
kind of antiseptic agent. Rummaging in the medicine chest, they
found sulfanilamide tablets and ground them to powder. One thing
was lacking: there was no means of holding open the wound after
the incision had been made. Surgical tools used for this are called
"muscular retractors." What would they use for retractors? There
was nothing in the medicine chest that gave the answer, so they
went as usual to the cook's galley.

In the galley they found tablespoons made of Monel metal. They  30
bent these at right angles and had their retractors.

Sterilizers? They went to one of the greasy copper-colored  31
torpedoes waiting beside the tubes. They milked alcohol from the
torpedo mechanism and used it as well as boiling water.

The light in the wardroom seemed insufficient; operating rooms  32
always have big lamps. So they brought one of the big floods used
for night loadings and rigged it inside the wardroom's sloping ceil-
ing.

33    The moment for the operation had come. Rector, very pale and stripped, stretched himself out on the wardroom table under the glare of the lamps.

34    Rubber gloves dipped in torpedo alcohol were drawn upon the youthful "Doc's" hands. The fingers were too long. The rubber ends dribbled limply over.

35    "You look like Mickey Mouse, Doc," said one onlooker.

36    Lipes grinned behind the gauze.

37    Rector on the wardroom table wet his lips, glancing a side look at the tea-strainer ether mask.

38    With his superior officers as his subordinates, Lipes looked into their eyes, nodded, and Hoskins put the tea mask down over Rector's face. No words were spoken; Hoskins already knew from the book that he should watch Rector's eye pupils dilate.

39    The twenty-three-year-old surgeon, following the ancient hand rule, put his little finger on Rector's subsiding umbilicus, his thumb on the point of the hipbone, and, by dropping his index finger straight down, found the point where he intended to cut. At his side stood Lieutenant Norvell Ward of Indian Head, Maryland, who was his assistant surgeon.

40    "I chose him for his coolness and dependability," said the Doc afterward of his superior officer. "He acted as my third and fourth hands."

41    Lieutenant Ward's job was to place tablespoons in Rector's side as Lipes cut through successive layers of muscles.

42    Engineering Officer Lieutenant S. Manning of Cheraw, South Carolina, took the job which in a normal operating room is known as "circulating nurse." His job was to see that packets of sterile dressings kept coming and that the torpedo alcohol and boiling water arrived regularly from the galley.

43    They had what is called an "instrument passer" in Chief Yeoman H. F. Wieg of Sheldon, North Dakota, whose job was to keep the tablespoons coming and coming clean. Submarine Skipper Ferrall too had his part. They made him "recorder." It was his job to keep count of the sponges that went into Rector. A double count of the tablespoons used as retractors was kept: one by the Skipper and one by the cook, who was himself passing them out from the galley.

44    It took Lipes in his flap-finger rubber gloves nearly twenty minutes to find the appendix.

"I have tried one side of the caecum," he whispered after the 45
first minutes. "Now, I'm trying the other."

Whispered bulletins seeped back into the engine room and the 46
crews' quarters.

"The Doc has tried one side of something and now is trying the 47
other side."

After more search, Lipes finally whispered, "I think I've got it. 48
It's curled way into the blind gut."

Lipes was using the classical McBurney's incision. Now was the 49
time when his shipmate's life was completely in his hands.

"Two more spoons." They passed the word to Lieutenant Ward. 50

"Two spoons at 14.45 hours [2:45 P.M.]," wrote Skipper Ferrall 51
on his note pad.

"More flashlights. And another battle lantern," demanded Lipes. 52

The patient's face, lathered with white petrolatum, began to 53
grimace.

"Give him more ether," ordered the Doc. 54

Hoskins looked doubtfully at the original five pounds of ether now 55
shrunk to hardly three quarters of one can, but once again the tea
strainer was soaked in ether. The fumes mounted up, thickening the
wardroom air and making the operating staff giddy.

"Want those blowers speeded up?" the Captain asked the Doc. 56

The blowers began to whir louder. 57

Suddenly came the moment when the Doc reached out his hand, 58
pointing toward the needle threaded with twenty-day chromic cat-
gut.

One by one the sponges came out. One by one the tablespoons 59
bent into right angles were withdrawn and returned to the galley.
At the end it was the skipper who nudged Lipes and pointed to the
tally of bent tablespoons. One was missing. Lipes reached into the
incision for the last time and withdrew the wishboned spoon and
closed the incision.

They even had the tool ready to cut off the thread. It was a pair 60
of fingernail scissors, well scalded in water and torpedo juice.

At that moment the last can of ether went dry. They lifted up 61
Rector and carried him into the bunk of Lieutenant Charles K.
Miller of Williamsport, Pennsylvania. Lieutenant Miller alone had
had control of the ship as diving officer during the operation.

62    It was half an hour after the last tablespoon had been withdrawn that Rector opened his eyes. His first words were, "I'm still in there pitching."

63    By that time the sweat-drenched officers were hanging up their pajamas to dry. It had taken the amateurs about two and a half hours for an operation ordinarily requiring forty-five minutes.

64    "It wasn't one of those 'snappy valve' appendixes," murmured Lipes apologetically as he felt the first handclasps upon his shoulders.

65    Within a few hours, the bow and stern planesmen, who, under Lieutenant Miller's direction, had kept the submarine from varying more than half a degree vertically in 150 minutes below the stormy sea, came around to receive Rector's winks of thanks. Rector's only remark was, "Gee, I wish Earl was here to see this job." His brother Earl, a seaman on the Navy submarine tender *Pigeon*, is among the list of missing at Corregidor, probably captured.

66    When the submarine surfaced that night, the ether-drunk submarine crewmen found themselves grabbing the sides of the conning tower and swaying unsteadily on their feet. Thirteen days later Rector, fully recovered, was at his battle station, manning the phones. In a bottle vibrating on the submarine's shelves was the prize exhibit of surgeon Lipes—the first appendix ever known to have been removed below enemy waters.

## Think about:

1.    the training, experience, and personality of Wheeler Lipes. In what ways—under the circumstances—was he a good choice of a person to act as the surgeon?

2.    the writer's use of the pronoun "they." Why does he repeat the word frequently, using it at the beginnings of sentences and paragraphs? What does this repetition suggest about the attitude and behavior of the group of people Weller is writing about?

3.      ways in which this was "probably the most democratic surgical operation ever performed." Consider, for example, the rank of each man in relation to his function during the operation.

## Write about:

an incident which you participated in or observed that required fast or careful action to solve an immediate problem. The incident might be a close call on the highway or elsewhere, a rescue from water, fire, or other danger, or even a less serious situation such as a particular moment in a game when decisive action was needed to win.

## Try out:

making your paper unified—as " 'Surgeon' in a Submarine" is unified—by emphasizing one main point all the way through. Note how Weller achieves **unity** by keeping the reader's attention focused throughout his narrative on the answer to one question: Will "they" be able to carry out the operation successfully? See if you can focus all through your story on the answer to a similar question.

Before you write, list on a scratch sheet in chronological order all the things that happened during the period you are writing about (see p. 13 on *chronological order*). You will be writing for someone who was not there, and your purpose will be to show the reader exactly what happened in the order that it happened, at the same time communicating the high level of interest or excitement you felt at the time. (Note that Weller does this, building suspense by telling step-by-step in detail what the people did to accomplish the job they were doing.) Because attention to detail will be especially important throughout your paper, your list will be a good guide for you as you write.

*Old Yeller, the Dog Who Knew When to Fight*

# Look for:

1.  what happens in this action-filled fictional story of life in Texas frontier country. A fictional story is one that is "made up." That is, it is a story whose characters and events a writer has created and written about. It is not a report about actual people and events. (See p. 29 on *fiction*.)

2.  the attitudes of the characters in this story—both people and animals—toward one another.

3.  these words:
    **lunging (LUNJ-ing)—leaping forward as in attack** [17]
    **rowdy (ROW-dee, pronounced ROW, to rhyme with how) —rough in a playful manner, noisy** [26]
    **romp (RAHMP)—a physically active playtime, free play not in an organized game** [26]

# Old Yeller, the Dog Who Knew When to Fight

**Fred Gipson**

I shouldered my axe and started toward the cabin, trying to think 1
up some excuse to tell Mama to keep her from knowing I was played
clear out.

That's when I heard Little Arliss scream. 2

Well, Little Arliss was a screamer by nature. He'd scream when 3
he was happy and scream when he was mad and a lot of times he'd
scream just to hear himself make a noise. Generally, we paid no more
mind to his screaming that we did to the gobble of a wild turkey.

But this time was different. The second I heard his screaming, I 4
felt my heart flop clear over. This time I knew Little Arliss was in
real trouble.

I tore out up the trail leading toward the cabin. A minute before, 5
I'd been so tired out with my rail splitting that I couldn't have struck
a trot. But now I raced through the tall trees in that creek bottom,
covering ground like a scared wolf.

Little Arliss's second scream, when it came, was louder and shriller 6
and more frantic-sounding than the first. Mixed with it was a
whimpering crying sound that I knew didn't come from him. It was
a sound I'd heard before and seemed like I ought to know what it
was, but right then I couldn't place it.

Then, from way off to one side came a sound that I would have 7
recognized anywhere. It was the coughing roar of a charging bear.
I'd just heard it once in my life. That was the time Mama had shot
and wounded a hog-killing bear and Papa had had to finish it off with
a knife to keep it from getting her.

My heart went to pushing up into my throat, nearly choking off 8
my wind. I strained for every lick of speed I could get out of my
running legs. I didn't know what sort of fix Little Arliss had got

himself into, but I knew that it had to do with a mad bear, which was enough.

9     The way the late sun slanted through the trees had the trail all cross-banded with streaks of bright light and dark shade. I ran through these bright and dark patches so fast that the changing light nearly blinded me. Then suddenly, I raced out into the open where I could see ahead. And what I saw sent a chill clear through to the marrow of my bones.

10    There was Little Arliss, down in that spring hole again. He was lying half in and half out of the water, holding onto the hind leg of a little black bear cub no bigger than a small coon. The bear cub was out on the bank, whimpering and crying and clawing the rocks with all three of his other feet, trying to pull away. But Little Arliss was holding on for all he was worth, scared now and screaming his head off. Too scared to let go.

11    How come the bear cub ever to prowl close enough for Little Arliss to grab him, I don't know. And why he didn't turn on him and bite loose, I couldn't figure out, either. Unless he was like Little Arliss, too scared to think.

12    But all of that didn't matter now. What mattered was the bear cub's mama. She'd heard the cries of her baby and was coming to save him. She was coming so fast that she had the brush popping and breaking as she crashed through and over it. I could see her black heavy figure piling off down the slant on the far side of Birdsong Creek. She was roaring mad and ready to kill.

13    And worst of all, I could see that I'd never get there in time!

14    Mama couldn't either. She'd heard Arliss, too, and here she came from the cabin, running down the slant toward the spring, screaming at Arliss, telling him to turn the bear cub loose. But Little Arliss wouldn't do it. All he'd do was hang with that hind leg and let out one shrill shriek after another as fast as he could suck in a breath.

15    Now the she bear was charging across the shallows in the creek. She was knocking sheets of water high in the bright sun, charging with her fur up and her long teeth bared, filling the canyon with that awful coughing roar. And no matter how fast Mama ran or how fast I ran, the she bear was going to get there first!

16    I think I nearly went blind then, picturing what was going to happen to Little Arliss. I know that I opened my mouth to scream and not any sound came out.

Then, just as the bear went lunging up the creek bank toward 17
Little Arliss and her cub, a flash of yellow came streaking out of the
brush.

It was that big yeller dog. He was roaring like a mad bull. He 18
wasn't one-third as big and heavy as the she bear, but when he piled
into her from one side, he rolled her clear off her feet. They went
down in a wild, roaring tangle of twisting bodies and scrambling feet
and slashing fangs.

As I raced past them, I saw the bear lunge up to stand on her hind 19
feet like a man while she clawed at the body of the yeller dog hanging
to her throat. I didn't wait to see more. Without ever checking my
stride, I ran in and jerked Little Arliss loose from the cub. I grabbed
him by the wrist and yanked him up out of that water and slung him
toward Mama like he was a half-empty sack of corn. I screamed at
Mama. "Grab him, Mama! Grab him and run!" Then I swung my
chopping axe high and wheeled, aiming to cave in the she bear's
head with the first lick.

But I never did strike. I didn't need to. Old Yeller hadn't let the 20
bear get close enough. He couldn't handle her; she was too big and
strong for that. She'd stand there on her hind feet, hunched over,
and take a roaring swing at him with one of those big front claws.
She'd slap him head over heels. She'd knock him so far that it didn't
look like he could possibly get back there before she charged again,
but he always did. He'd hit the ground rolling, yelling his head off
with the pain of the blow; but somehow he'd always roll to his feet.
And here he'd come again, ready to tie into her for another round.

I stood there with my axe raised, watching them for a long mo- 21
ment. Then from up toward the house, I heard Mama calling:
"Come away from there, Travis. Hurry, son! Run!"

That spooked me. Up till then, I'd been ready to tie into that bear 22
myself. Now, suddenly, I was scared out of my wits again. I ran
toward the cabin.

But like it was, Old Yeller nearly beat me there. I didn't see it, 23
of course; but Mama said that the minute Old Yeller saw we were
all in the clear and out of danger, he threw the fight to that she bear
and lit out for the house. The bear chased him for a little piece, but
at the rate Old Yeller was leaving her behind, Mama said it looked
like the bear was backing up.

But if the big yeller dog was scared or hurt in any way when he 24 came dashing into the house, he didn't show it. He sure didn't show it like we all did. Little Arliss had hushed his screaming, but he was trembling all over and clinging to Mama like he'd never let her go. And Mama was sitting in the middle of the floor, holding him up close and crying like she'd never stop. And me, I was close to crying, myself.

25    Old Yeller, though, all he did was come bounding in to jump on us and lick us in the face and bark so loud that there, inside the cabin, the noise nearly made us deaf.

26    The way he acted, you might have thought that bear fight hadn't been anything more than a rowdy romp that we'd all taken part in for the fun of it.

## Think about:

1.    exactly what Old Yeller did to save his people from the bear.

2.    what the bear was fighting for, what the dog was fighting for, and whether either of them won. Was there a hero? Was there a villain? What was the **conflict** about and how was it settled?

3.    the *climax* of the story. The **climax** of a narrative is the high point of the action; in a fictional narrative it is the scene in which the characters' problems are somehow settled. What scene seems to you to be the climax of this selection from the novel *Old Yeller?*

## Write about:

a fight or argument between any two or more opponents, animals or people, that you have witnessed or participated in. Show how the *conflict* began, what role each participant played in it, and how it was settled.

# Try out:

building up to the *climax* of your story with action-packed paragraphs, as Gipson does. Try starting directly by telling what you were doing (or what your character was doing) when the need for action arose. Tell step-by-step how one thing led to another. Again, you will be creating suspense as you did in the writing assignment for " 'Surgeon' in a Submarine." You will be planting in the reader's mind the question, "How is all this going to end?" and building up to an answer to that question. The answer will come in the climax. The climax can be the conclusion of your story, unless you decide that you need a sentence or two (like Gipson's last two paragraphs) to comment briefly on the way things worked out. Be sure that neither your concluding sentences nor any sentences in the body detract from the *unity* of your suspense-filled story. (Note that even the descriptive sentences in "Old Yeller" are used for the purpose of explaining or advancing action: The sentence "The way the late sun slanted through the trees had the trail all cross-banded with streaks of bright light and dark shade" is followed by "I ran through these bright and dark patches so fast that the changing light nearly blinded me.")

## The Most Important Day

# Look for:

1.      the way the first sentence states in a general way the main idea of the selection.

2.      Helen Keller's reasons for saying that March 3, 1887, was the most important day of her life.

3.      the meaning of the phrase "two lives" in the first paragraph. Why does Keller feel that she began a second life when Anne Sullivan came?

4.      a scene you can imagine being played on television. Perhaps you have in fact already seen the play or movie, *The Miracle Worker,* in which scenes from Helen Keller's life story are very dramatically presented.

5.      these words:

languor (LANG-g'r)—a feeling of being tired, unable to get into working or playing [2]

tangible (TAN-juh-b'l)—as used here, touchable, that is, capable of being touched (sometimes used to mean actual or real) [3]

plummet (PLUM-met)—a small but heavy metal object used to weigh down a line or rope. The plummet is used with the sounding line to measure depth of water. (These ship's tools were commonly used on old sailing vessels.) [3]

uncomprehending (un-com-pree-HEND-ing)—not understanding [5]

tussle (TUSS-s'l)—struggle, fight [6]

hearth (harth)—the area in front of a fireplace [6]

sentiment (SEN-tih-ment)—feeling, emotion [6]

# The Most Important Day

**Helen Keller**

The most important day I remember in all my life is the one 1
on which my teacher, Anne Mansfield Sullivan, came to me. I am
filled with wonder when I consider the immeasurable contrast between the two lives which it connects. It was the third of March,
1887, three months before I was seven years old.

On the afternoon of that eventful day, I stood on the porch, 2
dumb, expectant. I guessed vaguely from my mother's signs and
from the hurrying to and fro in the house that something unusual
was about to happen, so I went to the door and waited on the steps.
The afternoon sun penetrated the mass of honeysuckle that covered
the porch and fell on my upturned face. My fingers lingered almost
unconsciously on the familiar leaves and blossoms which had just
come forth to greet the sweet southern spring. I did not know what
the future held of marvel or surprise for me. Anger and bitterness
had preyed upon me continually for weeks and a deep languor had
succeeded this passionate struggle.

Have you ever been at sea in a dense fog, when it seemed as if 3
a tangible white darkness shut you in, and the great ship, tense and
anxious, groped her way toward the shore with plummet and sounding-line, and you waited with beating heart for something to happen? I was like that ship before my education began, only I was
without compass or sounding-line, and had no way of knowing how
near the harbour was. "Light! give me light!" was the wordless cry
of my soul, and the light of love shone on me in that very hour.

I felt approaching footsteps. I stretched out my hand as I sup- 4
posed to my mother. Some one took it, and I was caught up and held
close in the arms of her who had come to reveal all things to me,
and, more than all things else, to love me.

The morning after my teacher came she led me into her room and 5

From *The Story of My Life*. New York: Doubleday, 1902.

gave me a doll. The little blind children at the Perkins Institution had sent it and Laura Bridgman had dressed it; but I did not know this until afterward. When I had played with it a little while, Miss Sullivan slowly spelled into my hand the word "d-o-l-l." I was at once interested in this finger play and tried to imitate it. When I finally succeeded in making the letters correctly I was flushed with childish pleasure and pride. Running downstairs to my mother I held up my hand and made the letters for doll. I did not know that I was spelling a word or even that words existed; I was simply making my fingers go in monkey-like imitation. In the days that followed I learned to spell in this uncomprehending way a great many words, among them *pin, hat, cup* and a few verbs like *sit, stand* and *walk.* But my teacher had been with me several weeks before I understood that everything has a name.

6    One day, while I was playing with my new doll, Miss Sullivan put my big rag doll into my lap also spelled "d-o-l-l" and tried to make me understand that "d-o-l-l" applied to both. Earlier in the day we had had a tussle over the words "m-u-g" and "w-a-t-e-r." Miss Sullivan had tried to impress it upon me that "m-u-g" is *mug* and that "w-a-t-e-r" is *water,* but I persisted in confounding the two. In despair she had dropped the subject for the time, only to renew it at the first opportunity. I became impatient at her repeated attempts and, seizing the new doll, I dashed it upon the floor. I was keenly delighted when I felt the fragments of the broken doll at my feet. Neither sorrow nor regret followed my passionate outburst. I had not loved the doll. In the still, dark world in which I lived there was no strong sentiment or tenderness. I felt my teacher sweep the fragments to one side of the hearth, and I had a sense of satisfaction that the cause of my discomfort was removed. She brought me my hat, and I knew I was going out into the warm sunshine. This thought, if a wordless sensation may be called a thought, made me hop and skip with pleasure.

7    We walked down the path to the well-house, attracted by the fragrance of the honeysuckle with which it was covered. Some one was drawing water and my teacher placed my hand under the spout. As the cool stream gushed over one hand she spelled into the other the word *water,* first slowly, then rapidly. I stood still, my whole attention fixed upon the motions of her fingers. Suddenly I felt a misty consciousness as of something forgotten—a thrill of returning

thought; and somehow the mystery of language was revealed to me. I knew then that "w-a-t-e-r" meant the wonderful cool something that was flowing over my hand. That living word awakened my soul, gave it light, hope, joy, set it free! There were barriers still, it is true, but barriers that could in time be swept away.

I left the well-house eager to learn. Everything had a name, and 8 each name gave birth to a new thought. As we returned to the house every object which I touched seemed to quiver with life. That was because I saw everything with the strange, new sight that had come to me. On entering the door I remembered the doll I had broken. I felt my way to the hearth and picked up the pieces. I tried vainly to put them together. Then my eyes filled with tears; for I realized what I had done, and for the first time I felt repentance and sorrow.

I learned a great many new words that day. I do not remember 9 what they all were; but I do know that *mother, father, sister, teacher* were among them—words that were to make the world blossom for me, "like Aaron's rod, with flowers." It would have been difficult to find a happier child than I was as I lay in my crib at the close of that eventful day and lived over the joys it had brought me, and for the first time longed for a new day to come.

## Think about:

1.    Helen Keller's reasons for saying that the day Anne Sullivan came to stay with her was the most important day of her life. Note that three different days are discussed in this account. As you reread the selection, number each of these days as you come to the paragraph or paragraphs telling about it. Why do you suppose Keller believes that the first of these days was the most important one? If you were writing this account, which of the three days would you say was the most important? Why? How does Keller achieve *unity* here even though she writes about three different incidents occurring on three different days? (See p. 66 for more on *unity.*)

2.  the author's statement that the incident at the pump "revealed the mystery of language" to her. What exactly does she learn about language through this incident?

3.  in what ways the incident at the pump changes Helen's attitudes and behavior. Compare, for example, the way she feels about her broken doll after this experience with the way she felt at the time she broke it.

4.  Keller's imaginative uses of language. Note especially her extended metaphor (p. 74) in which she compares herself to a ship lost in the fog. Why is this comparison especially appropriate? How does her expression "white darkness" make sense the way she uses it here?

## Write about:

a time when you discovered something about your own capabilities. The discovery need not be an earthshaking one, and the day it happened need not have been "the most important day" in your life. But choose an incident you like to remember because of the thrill of accomplishment you associate with it. Maybe it was the time you first went out with someone of the opposite sex and discovered you were attractive and interesting. Or maybe it was the night you finally solved an algebra problem without someone else's help and began to enjoy math as a game you could win at. Or maybe it was way back when you first managed to play volleyball without falling down and realized you were going to develop some balance and coordination after all.

## Try out:

writing a paper of several paragraphs, developing a main idea all the way through as Keller does. Since your story may be considerably shorter than Keller's, you may not need as many paragraphs as she has. But for a paper like this—one in which you develop an idea about an experience—you should have a short introductory paragraph, at least one body paragraph, and a brief paragraph that brings the story to a conclusion. (See p. 13 for more on *introduction, body,* and *conclusion.*)

Note that in Keller's introductory paragraph, the first sentence states directly the main idea of the entire piece of writing. This kind of sentence is called a **thesis sentence.** Like the topic sentence of a paragraph, it is usually the most general sentence in the work. Although the thesis sentence of an essay or story often appears in the first paragraph, it need not be the first sentence of that paragraph. However, you may find it helpful this time to begin with a thesis sentence as Keller does. This will be a good way of helping yourself to achieve unity in your story. (See p. 66 on *unity.*) You will establish for yourself and for your reader at the very beginning the point you want to emphasize throughout.

You may want a more casual introduction than Keller's thesis sentence, however. You might try something like, "I've never forgotten the night Fred came home from his trip to Africa," or "One of the big moments of my junior year in high school was the time I got an award for achievement in basketball."

In your body paragraphs, you should concentrate on showing the reader exactly what happened that gave you a new perspective on your abilities. Note that only in the first and last sentences does Keller *talk about* the importance of the event; the rest of the time she *shows* you what happened to make the incident important to her. In other words, she gives a very detailed account of her experiences. (Note, for example, the details the author includes in ¶6 that show how she learned that words name things.) In your story, see if you can show both what happened and why it was important— through similar use of details.

Then, when you come to your concluding paragraph, you can be very brief. You will simply want to find a way to come back quickly to the idea of your thesis sentence without necessarily saying exactly the same thing you said in your introduction. Keller does this by speaking at the end about the *joy* that Anne Sullivan brought into her life to reinforce the idea she introduced at the beginning about the *importance* of the teacher's arrival.

# EXPOSITION

*Get Out on a Limb!*

## Look for:

1.   the way the title signals the content of the article and the attitude of the writer toward his subject. As the first two sentences show, the title phrase "get out on a limb" is to be taken literally, that is, the writer tells the reader to go up in a tree. But is there any way in which the old saying about "getting out on a limb"—meaning taking a chance—makes sense here?

2.   the variety of wildlife that the author tells of seeing while perched in a tree.

3.   these words:
   **pell-mell (PEL MEL)—in a rush, as in a stampede, in a confused way—not a deliberate way** [1]

   **camouflage (KAM-uh-flazj)—disguise, a deliberate attempt to hide something** [3]

   **bizarre (b'-ZAR)—unusual, strange, weird** [5]

   **rutting (RUT-ting)—state of sexual excitement, particularly in large mammals. (The rutting season means the mating season. "In rut" means in heat.)** [10]

# Get Out on a Limb!

Glenn Helgeland

At first, nothing much happens. But after a while, little by little,   1
the wildlife you frightened away when you climbed up into your
perch in that tree starts coming back. Motionless, you scan every
square foot of forest floor below and see a shrew, threading a pell-
mell course over some fallen leaves. Glancing upward, you catch the
fleeting, climb-and-stall airplane glide of a downy woodpecker as it
lands on a nearby tree. Moments later, you hear a rustling in the
underbrush, followed by the high-pitched peeping of a ruffled
grouse. As it emerges, jerkily stretching its neck back and forth, the
bird suddenly cocks its head in your direction and, apparently
alarmed, takes four quick steps and bursts into flight.

Sitting in a tree, 12 to 15 feet or more above the ground, may   2
seem like a crazy way to spend an afternoon. But if you're the kind
of person who loves to watch wildlife, it could prove to be the
ultimate nature experience. It certainly has, on many occasions, been
just that for me.

The pastime is not without its problems. The first of these is   3
finding a tree in a good location that you can indeed climb into.
Then, once you are up there, the trick is to avoid detection—
through camouflage and other means—by the very animals you want
to see. A third problem is the danger of falling *out* of your tree. That
may seem improbable enough, but drowsing—especially on a warm,
relaxing day—can lead to a fall. All of these difficulties are manage-
able, though, and the rewards of getting out on a limb are usually
well worth the effort.

I began observing wildlife from trees while bowhunting for deer.   4
Consequently, my tree-sitting outfit includes many ideas borrowed
from that sport: a camouflage jacket, cap and trousers, with the
jacket buttoned to the top so the skin at my neck doesn't show. Light

skin is one of the most glaringly out-of-place color tones in any outdoor setting. The backs of my hands, my face, nose, eyelids, forehead and neck above the jacket are all smeared with black cream. The cap covers my hair. The wire rims on my eyeglasses are covered with black, nonreflective tape and, to avoid reflection from the lenses, I will sit facing away from the sun whenever possible. In addition, I make certain that my belt buckle is concealed beneath my jacket, and that my wristwatch and wedding ring are removed.

5    Decked out in this bizarre costume, I usually head off into the woods with a pretty good idea of where I want to go. Though tree selection is often a case of trial and error, it's wise to get situated near game trails and potential feeding areas. Often, this means finding a tree where two types of habitat converge—where a woodland meets a marsh, for example. Always select a tree that is downwind of the area you will be watching, so the animals do not pick up your scent. Then, stay in that tree for several hours. Don't hop from one tree to another every 20 minutes. Though it's possible to spend an entire day there without seeing too much wildlife, it's best to be patient. If one area doesn't work, try another the next time out.

6    One of my most memorable incidents took place one autumn afternoon, while I was perched in a tall oak tree close to a swamp and an alfalfa field. Evidently, both of those areas were good hunting territory for owls. Just as deep dusk was setting in, I heard the hard whisper of wind above me. In the nick of time, I looked up to startle a great-horned owl into shifting its landing plans to another oak. Apparently, it had mistaken my stocking-capped head for an ideal stump upon which to land.

7    In these same woods, my wife spent a fall day sitting in another tall oak, admiring the leaves as they dropped from nearby trees. Suddenly, it dawned on her that those extrawide leaves were not only falling—they were also reattaching themselves to other trees. They were flying squirrels, a large family of them, leaping and gliding from tree to tree—including the one my wife was in.

8    Deer are by far the most fascinating creatures to watch. They are known as "dumb" creatures of habit but I've seen them outsmart the most "expert" outdoorsman. If you have the time over the course of a summer and fall, you can watch from a tree as the fawns grow and gradually become wiser to the ways of the woods. You also

quickly learn that an old doe is just as smart—if not smarter—than the admired buck.

Not long ago, I met another wildlife watcher who had just spent a Saturday afternoon in a tree and was still buzzing about what he had seen. Shortly after he had gotten settled, a doe and two fawns entered the area and headed straight for the base of his tree. There, they bedded down, just a few feet below the onlooker. "Have you ever held your breath and not blinked your eyes for 45 minutes?" he asked me. 9

During rutting season in the fall, some tree-sitters use a deer musk scent on their clothes to cover their own odor. One Nebraskan told me about an experience he had while watching a coyote hunt for gophers in a field near the tree where he was seated. Earlier, he had dropped some deer scent on the soles of his shoes about 50 yards from the tree. "Suddenly," he recalled, "the coyote picked up the scent and made a beeline for the tree. Before I knew it, it had its paws up against the trunk and was carefully looking over every branch. The whole time, its nostrils were working like suction pumps. I kept perfectly still and eventually it gave up trying to figure out how a deer had gotten up into that tree. It trotted off, looked back once and returned to the gopher field." 10

Another friend of mine tried the same technique in a Wisconsin forest, and wound up attracting a doe to his tree. "My feet were only about six feet off the ground," he told me, "and as she stood there, I could see that her eyes were glossed-over as she concentrated on the scent. Her nose was only about 14 inches from my toe, but she didn't see it—or me. Then I scraped my foot on the bark and she almost fell down trying to get away." 11

The highlight of all my own treesitting has to do with deer, too. After waiting for what seemed like an eternity one afternoon, I finally heard a telltale sound. 12

*Tick.* A fallen leaf was disturbed, behind me and to my left. A deer trail was in that direction. 13

*Tick.* Another step, another leaf. Then silence, except for my heart beating. Since the tree trunk masked me from any creature approaching from my left, I turned my head to be ready. My eyes involuntarily darted left as I turned and immediately I saw them: five whitetail does. 14

15    They slowly fed past me, only 14 yards away. It seemed as if everything was happening in slow motion. The deer were so close, I felt pinned against the tree.

16    Suddenly, they broke into a curving dash off the trail and into thick underbrush. They milled around a few seconds, then dashed in an arc into thicker brush, where all five stopped dead still. I had heard about this playful behavior during rut. Now I had seen it. But where was the buck?

17    After several minutes of absolute stillness, I heard a steady scuffing of leaves from the direction in which the does had approached. A spike buck, young and eager, walked swiftly into view, head down, sniffing the earth, trailing the does. Quickly, it passed my tree, curved off where the does had made their arc, paused where they first stopped, then quickly scuffed out of sight, still on their trail.

18    Deer in rut will move at any time of the day and with less caution than at other times of the year. Most likely, this buck was only an observer that year; bigger, more mature males would probably send him packing.

19    An hour or so later, with dusk falling, I heard the slow, irregular pace of something else moving through the woods. I remained still, hoping it would pass close enough to permit identification. Sure enough, the animal moved past and paused on a small ridge, giving me a good look at its silhouette. Then, it plodded out of sight beyond the ridge.

20    That last animal never even suspected that it was being watched. Part of it had to do with the lengthening shadows and my effective camouflage. But I have discovered, over the years, that—like most other big creatures—the human animal rarely looks up into a tree.

## Think about:

1.    the author's preparation for a wildlife-watching expedition. What steps does he take to get ready?

2.    his inactivity as the way he deliberately chooses to behave in this situation. What difficulties does he have in staying absolutely still? How does his stillness get him what he wants?

3.    the contrast between the way a wildlife-watcher acts and the way a person goes about almost any other outdoor sport or activity. What would a hiker or biker in the same territory experience that Helgeland does not? What would the hiker or biker miss out on?

## Write about:

how you go about doing something that is of special interest or of practical importance to you. You might write about a hobby of yours or a job you have held: lifeguarding, paramedic or rescue work, building or rebuilding a fast car, photographing birds or animals, collecting rocks and gems, or waiting on tables in a fine restaurant, for example. At any rate, it will be something you can do that not everyone knows how to do. Your purpose will be to tell readers how *you* do whatever it is you are writing about in order that they can decide whether this is something they would like to learn to do, too. Assume that your readers have very little knowledge of whatever you are writing about.

## Try out:

first, remembering exactly what steps you took to carry out the activity the last time you did it. Next, list these steps (actions) in the order in which they occurred. Then decide whether, because of unexpected happenings, some of these steps were done differently this time from the way you usually do them; if so, cross the odd happenings off your list. Finally, list either the advantages of your method or the rewards of the activity you are describing.

You will now have the basis for an **outline** that will fit this three-part organization:

I. Preparations (buying or assembling tools and materials, for example)
II. Methods of carrying out the activity
III. Rewards or advantages

Under each of the first two headings, list the things you usually do or the steps you usually take, drawing from your first list. Note that although you probably used the past tense in that list (I said, I did, I found), in writing this outline you will want to use the present tense (I say, I do, I find). You will be talking about what you usually do, not about what you did at one particular time. This method of organization will not be exactly like Helgeland's, as he uses a problems–solutions–rewards structure, but this organization (preparation–methods–rewards) will be a useful one for you to follow in preparing your "How to Do It" essay.

The categories of your outline will make up the *body* of your paper. You will need several paragraphs in the body—one for "preparations" and probably more than one for "methods of carrying out the activity." This means that you will need to give particular attention to getting from one paragraph to another—that is, to **transitions.** Note that Helgeland uses various *transitional phrases* at the beginnings of paragraphs to link up one paragraph with the next. Some of these, for example, "Not long ago" (¶9) and "During rutting season in the Fall" (¶10) take the reader from one time period to another. And some others, "Decked out in this bizarre costume" (¶5) and "In these same woods" (¶7), refer back to the last sentence of the preceding paragraph. You will probably find that transitional techniques like these will work for you in your paper.

Some additional transitional words that you may find useful in this *chronologically* organized paper are "next," "then," "afterwards," "from time to time," and "finally." You may think of others.

Even within paragraphs, transitional words and phrases

that link sentences can be useful. Note, for example, Helgeland's use of time-noting words and phrases within paragraphs—"Before I knew it" (¶10), "Earlier," (¶10), and "Suddenly" (¶10). Use of transitional words and phrases like these within paragraphs is one way of giving your paragraphs **coherence,** that is, making the parts of your paragraphs stick together as you develop your topic sentences.

Paragraph 3 of "Get Out on a Limb" is an excellent example of both *topic sentence* development and the use of *transitional* words and phrases to tie the parts of the paragraph together. The first sentence, "The pastime is not without its problems" is clearly the topic sentence, as such *general* sentences usually are. And phrases like "the first of these," "then," and "a third problem" tie together the examples of the problems that the first sentence mentions. This paragraph can serve as a good model for your own paragraph development.

Of course this paper, like your last one, should have not only a well-organized, detailed body but appropriate, brief introductory and concluding paragraphs as well. One purpose of your introductory paragraph will be to interest the reader in learning to do whatever it is you are writing about. Note that Helgeland gets his readers' attention by giving them interesting glimpses of wildlife he has experienced on a typical "watch." And note that his last paragraph very smoothly brings the reader back to the point he had started out with, that is, that all kinds of animals—humans included —can be observed if the watcher follows the instructions he provides. Try to bring your paper to a similarly brief and clinching conclusion.

*Indian School: It Was Whispered on the Wind*

# Look for:

1.  the writer's attitude toward the Navajos and the way he expresses this attitude through his choice of language. Note especially the subtitle and the wording of the first paragraph.

2.  the way the man who is the subject of this article demonstrates his attitudes toward his Indian neighbors.

3.     the Navajos' attitude toward Ryan. Do they view him as different from other white people of their experience? Why or why not?

4.     these words:

    **buttes (BEWTS, like "beaut" in "beautiful")—isolated cliffs** [1]

    **solemnity (sol-EM-n'-tee)—seriousness. (Think of the adjective "solemn.")** [5]

    **hogans (HO-g'nz)—traditional houses built by Navajo Indians** [14]

    **consummate (con-SUM-met)—perfect, ending in achievement and satisfaction. An adjective. You may know the verb "consummate" (CON-sum-mate) meaning to complete.** [17]

    **linear accelerator (LIN-ee-'r ack-SELL-er-A-t'r)—a device in which charged particles are propelled fast in a straight line** [19]

    **legendary (LEDGE-'n-dare-ee)—according to story, song, or folktale** [23]

    **traumatic (trah-MAT-ik or traw-MAT-ik)—harmful, causing great physical or emotional pain** [31]

    **nuclear fusion (NOOK-lee-'r FEW-zjon)—the union of atomic nuclei, resulting in the release of great quantities of energy** [34]

    **geodesics (gee-o-DEE-sicks)—the principles of building geodesic domes, hollow shapes composed of many triangular pieces** [41]

    **apathy (AP-path-ee)—lack of feeling and energy** [44]

    **providential (prahv-ih-DENT-ch'l)—happening as though by a sudden act of God or Providence; lucky** [47]

    **emphatic (em-FAT-ik)—definite, forceful, and often loud and sudden as well** [65]

# Indian School: It Was Whispered on the Wind

Al Martinez

1    The Navajos call the wind ni-yol and believe that it blows down from the buttes and across the flat desert to awaken the trees and wildflowers from their long winter sleep.

2    Older Indians give it spiritual properties and say that the voices of spirits from the past ride the Southwest breezes and whisper to them, offering advice and help.

3    One of the voices they hear is that of the medicine man Hataali Yaazhe, Little Singer. It comes to them at the dawn prayer by the Little Colorado River, and sometimes as they ride horseback through the quiet beauty of the Painted Desert.

4    Little Singer whispers to them, "Bring our children home."

5    Polly Curley tells the story in a hogan on the Navajo reservation just north of Winslow. She tells it with great solemnity, for she is the daughter of Hataali Yaazhe, and the memory is sacred.

6    "What my father wanted more than anything is that the Navajo culture not die," she says, ". . . that the language of our people be preserved and spoken, and that the children of Birdsprings be brought home to learn."

7    Sitting across from her, 35-year-old Tom Ryan—a bearded, 6-foot-4 nuclear physicist, blood brother to the Navajos—listens respectfully.

8    "The spirits brought Tom Ryan to us," Polly Curley says, nodding toward him, "and the wish of Hataali Yaazhe comes true."

9    The "wish" is a pair of striking geodesic domes that rise from the red-sand desert floor 100 feet behind the hogan. They call it Little Singer School.

10    It probably will open for the first time in September, and at least 30 of the young children of Birdsprings will no longer be taken from their parents and sent off to federal boarding schools.

And no one in Birdsprings seems particularly surprised that a 11 Navajo medicine man and a Long Beach-born nuclear physicist made it happen.

Long before the construction of the school even began, it was 12 whispered on the wind. . . .

The Navajo reservation, largest in the United States, sprawls over 13 25,000 square miles of land in Arizona, New Mexico, Utah and Colorado.

Birdsprings sits in the high desert 22 miles north of Winslow, and 14 is a community of 560 Navajos living in hogans and a few drab houses on a small corner of the reservation occupied by 120,000 Indians.

Ryan was attracted to the climate of northeastern Arizona seven 15 years ago to improve the health of an ailing son, to write a book and to escape the pain of a shattered marriage.

He had not intended it to be a permanent stay. He had no 16 knowledge of, and held no particular interest in, the Navajos or their problems.

Ryan had saved $15,000 and had brought with him to Winslow 17 the equipment for gravitational research, one of his many pursuits. He was the consummate scientist, living in a world of theories and symbols, able to communicate his ideas with only a handful of other scientists throughout the world.

Since graduating from UC Berkeley in 1960, he had buried him- 18 self in satellite research, nuclear engineering, low-temperature phys- ics and missile systems development, both for the government and private industry.

When he was only 18, he built a linear accelerator and won 19 national acclaim for predicting the effect of the Van Allen radiation belt on rocket fuel.

Why he was attracted to the Navajos remains something of a 20 mystery even to Ryan, whose scientific disciplines are as far removed from their culture as space travel to herbal magic.

He talks about it as he drives along the rutted dirt roads of the 21 Indian Nation, and across the dry bed of the Little Colorado, where the leaves of the cottonwood trees shimmer in the wind and the bristly young tamaracks awaken to spring.

His first friend in Birdsprings was Grandpa Earl Johnson, a mem- 22 ber of the Tribal Council, then Dennis Nez, with whom he would someday become blood brother.

23   It was Grandpa Earl who took Ryan to meet Little Singer, an aging and wrinkled medicine man of the Tangle Clan, whose spiritual powers were legendary among the Navajos.

24   He was drawn to Little Singer, and Little Singer to Ryan. They spoke for long hours in Hataali Yaazhe's earth-and-timber hogan and at pow-wows around a campfire.

25   The medicine man invited the physicist to a "sing"—prayer ceremonies that sometimes last for days—and told him about the culture of the Navajos.

26   For a white man to be invited to a sing was a rare occasion, but it was even rarer that his life would become so deeply entwined with the dreams of an ancient culture.

27   "As I became involved in the community," Ryan says, "I began to realize that I hadn't seen many school-aged children, and I wondered where they were.

28   "Little Singer told me they were off at boarding schools run by the Bureau of Indian Affairs, and that sometimes the parents didn't see them for months . . . little ones from 6 years on up.

29   "I learned that they were raised in a mostly Anglo culture at the schools, and that while it is less harsh now, at one time the teachers wouldn't even let them speak the Navajo language.

30   "Little Singer told me, 'They are killing our culture' . . ."

31   He found the separation is traumatic—especially for parents without cars or other means of transportation, who can afford to visit their children only infrequently.

32   "What affected me deeply," Ryan says, "was when one of the fathers asked me to drive his 6-year-old daughter off to boarding school.

33   "She cried and screamed as though her heart would break. Tears came to my eyes. It was painful seeing her taken from her parents, a child so small and so lonesome . . .

34   "I was doing theoretical work in nuclear fusion at the time. I began thinking, why should the world have this advanced source of power when a basic fundamental is ignored? If we can't care for the children of Birdsprings, is what I'm doing worth it?"

35   He remembered that once he had attended a one-room schoolhouse. Why not, he wondered, a schoolhouse here?

He pursued that possibility. A first contact with the Bureau of 36
Indian Affairs proved negative. The BIA wasn't interested in the
idea.

The Navajo Tribal Council said it was up to the community of 37
Birdsprings. If they wanted a school, he could try to get one built
. . . but he would have to raise the money.

That was in 1971. "Little Singer told me he would say certain 38
prayers," Ryan recalls. "He said that there could be no community
without the children, that even the sacred songs were being forgotten."

At first, most of the Indians were suspicious of the physicist's 39
motives. "Why would an Anglo want to come in and help us?" Polly
Curley asks gravely. "They never have before."

But Ryan was not to be put off. Already he was trying to come 40
up with a design for the school. And then:

"I was riding a horse through the Painted Desert, a holy place, 41
when the design came to me. It was clear as anything I had ever
conceived, though I had no background in geodesics."

What emerged on paper was the domed, hogan-like structure that 42
symbolizes, in Navajo tradition, earth, life and universe.

Translating dream to substance, however, takes time, and Ryan 43
meanwhile was running out of living money. He had to accept a job
teaching engineering at Northern Arizona University in nearby
Flagstaff, just to keep the rent paid and food on the table.

Little Singer, in a quiet way, did his part. Whenever the physicist 44
faced suspicion or apathy, the medicine man would tell him to go
forward, that the school would be built.

When the job in Flagstaff ended, Ryan moved on to another— 45
this time at Foothill College on the San Francisco Peninsula.

While he was gone, Little Singer died quietly in his sleep. 46

This too seemed providential to the scientist, the triggering force 47
that turned an idea into reality. He began telling his students and
fellow faculty members about the Birdspring school project, and the
response was electric.

In a very short time, they had contributed $5,000. 48

Meanwhile, Polly Curley was leading a community effort on the 49
reservation to set aside 60 acres of sacred ground—land where the
medicine man had once chanted—for a school.

Little Singer had told her before he died that Ryan was the man 50 who would get the school built, and who would bring their children home.

51    Convinced by now that Ryan's intentions were honorable, she flew to California (her first plane ride) and told the students and faculty of Foothill College how much the school meant.

52    This time, more than money was forthcoming. Twenty-three of Ryan's students volunteered to come to Birdsprings to help build the school.

53    Work began in the summer of 1976.

54    When the Foothill money was used up, Ryan gave $7,000 from his own savings. When that was gone, he pursued—and got—a $5,000 grant from the Packard Foundation.

55    The work wasn't easy. There is no electricity on the reservation, and when their one generator broke down early in the building process, everything had to be done by hand.

56    Navajos worked side by side with the students, digging, sawing, laying 43,000 pounds of concrete blocks. Money began to come from the Tribal Council, and also from Ryan's father, himself a scientist.

57    Ryan by then had landed a job not too far away as an engineer for the Bechtel Corp.'s Los Angeles-based Power Division, which was building a fossil fuel plant at Cholla.

58    Still he devoted, and devotes, weekends, holidays and evenings to the school.

59    It remains uncompleted, and there is no money for the remainder of the work, but that doesn't bother Ryan.

60    He is convinced it will open in September for students in grades one to three, and that each year another room will be added.

61    But before classes begin in Birdsprings, the community must raise another $20,000 for the remaining basic work—$50,000 if they want the "luxuries" of plumbing and heating.

62    Thereafter, there will be two teachers (bilingual) and two teaching assistants to pay. The dream goes on.

63    Ryan is satisfied that it will work out. "I promised Little Singer that the children would be brought home," he says, "and they will be."

64    Is the school important to the Navajos?

65    Dale and Evelyn Dixon, both born on the reservation and both products of boarding schools, answer an emphatic yes. They have children ages 6, 8, and 9 at public schools in Winslow.

Rather than have them attend boarding schools, the Dixons  66
moved "to town" so they would not be parted from their three little
ones. They consider it the lesser of two evils.

"The reservation is our home," Dixon said. "It is where our soul  67
is. But we couldn't stand to be away from the children. Boarding
schools are prison camps, and my children will not go to prison
camps."

Dixon remembers when he was in boarding school that his mouth  68
was washed out with soap if he even spoke Navajo. A teacher there
complained, "What's wrong with you kids? You won't stop talking
Indian!"

"If this were an Anglo problem," Dale adds, "they would never  69
allow boarding schools to take their children away for months at a
time. They would be out there with guns."

Ryan intends that Birdsprings will be his home.  70

"I came here for a year," he says, sitting in the hogan near the  71
geodesic domes, "and I will stay forever."

He pauses. "But sometimes, I wonder how it all happened."  72

Polly Curley, daughter of the medicine man Hataali Yaazhe, says  73
nothing. She smiles to herself, takes another chaw of tobacco, and
listens to the wind.

## Think about:

1. the writer's use of the word "wind" in poetic phrases
throughout this article (¶¶ 12, 21, and 73, for example).
Why does Martinez stress this word? What does the wind
mean to the Navajos?

2. how the writer helps the reader to understand the Navajos'
feelings and needs. What phrases and ideas from their culture does he introduce? What descriptions of their homeland
show that Martinez puts himself in their place?

3.     how the writer shows the physicist's growing sympathy with the Navajos and their cause—and how he shows the Navajos growing to trust Ryan. What phrases of Tom's or Polly's show these understandings coming about?

4.     the length of the paragraphs in this selection. Note that some paragraphs are very short; ¶¶ 12, 19, and 40, for example, consist of only one sentence each. The reason for this brevity is that the selection appeared originally as a newspaper article. Because newspapers are prepared for rapid reading, newspaper writers often write brief, eye-catching paragraphs. This practice is accepted as standard journalistic style. However, in writing that is not intended for a newspaper, a better practice is the one you have been learning: beginning each paragraph with a topic sentence and then developing that topic fully.

## Write about:

a specific accomplishment of someone you admire and respect. This person should be either someone you know well or someone you interview specifically for the purpose of getting information for this paper. Perhaps you have a relative who has succeeded in business or a friend who has performed an unusual service for the community. Or you may know that one of your professors has done some original scientific experiments or has composed and published music. Perhaps you may have heard of someone not very far away who collects unusual stamps and knows a great deal about the history of the countries they represent. Since this may be the first paper you have written that is about someone else's feelings, interests, opinions, and actions, you will want to make a particular effort to be accurate and fair. That is, you will want to make sure that you do not confuse your own feelings and opinions with those of the person you are writing about.

## Try out:

listing the questions you hope to have the person answer. Even if you know the person well, it will be a good idea to conduct an interview for the purpose of getting specific answers to particular questions. If you prepare these questions in a logical order and note down the answers in this same order, you will have the basis of an outline for your paper. You might start your interview with questions about the person's early life and education, and then lead in to questions about the particular accomplishment you are interested in. Then, when you go over your notes, you can decide how much of the background material is really necessary to help the reader understand the person's accomplishment. You can leave out unnecessary information when you prepare your final outline. The headings of that outline might be:

    I. Early life
    II. Major accomplishment
    III. Results or significance of that accomplishment
(See p. 85 for a discussion of outlines.)

In your last two papers you wrote an introduction, body, and conclusion, weaving them with transitional words and phrases into a coherent whole. Plan this paper similarly, attracting your reader's interest in your opening statement, then getting across important information about the person you have interviewed, and finally coming to a conclusion that brings the reader back to your basic reason for being interested in this person and his or her accomplishment.

*The Internal Combustion Engine*

# Look for:

1. the writer's factual, totally unemotional treatment of the functioning of an automobile engine.

2. the way the writer helps you to understand the facts of the engine's functioning by leading you from one step in the process to the next.

3. these words:

   **motive (MO-tiv)—a reason for doing something** [1]

   **ignite (ig-NITE)—set fire to** [2]

   **dissipate (DISS-sih-pate)—scatter and cause to disappear (or seem to do so)** [2]

   **induction (in-DUCK-shun)—taking in. ("Induction" into the army has the same meaning.)** [4]

   **abrasive (uh-BRAY-siv)—rubbing in a manner that wears something down** [8]

*also:* any technical terms concerning the parts of an automobile engine that you do not fully understand. Note that the writer explains the functioning of these parts as he shows how the engine works. But you may want fuller information about the appearance and structure of the objects that these terms refer to. A good automotive manual —with illustrations—can give you some help. You can also consult a good dictionary.

# The Internal Combustion Engine

**Athan Constantin**

An internal combustion engine powers our modern automobile. 1
The engine burns its fuel within the engine proper, as compared to
a steam engine where the fuel is burned externally. The gasoline and
air mixture of the internal combustion engine is compressed by a
piston inside an airtight cylinder and ignited by a spark. The trapped
air-fuel mixture burns fiercely, causing tremendous heat which ex-
pands the trapped gases and pushes the piston down. This is the
motive power of our automobile.

The automobile engine is essentially a heat engine. It requires fuel 2
to burn, a spark to ignite the fuel, lubrication to minimize friction,
and a cooling system to dissipate unwanted heat.

It takes a correctly proportioned mixture of gasoline and air to 3
burn and develop the power needed to push the piston down the
cylinder. To store, mix, and deliver this air-fuel mixture is the duty
of the fuel system.

Gasoline is brought to the carburetor from a tank by a fuel pump. 4
Filtered air is drawn through the carburetor by the "sucking" action
of the pistons as they move downward in the cylinders, creating a
low-pressure area above them. The resulting pressure differential
causes the outside air, under normal atmospheric pressure, to move
through the induction system. As it passes through the carburetor,
it causes gasoline to be sprayed from the jets. This fine liquid mist
mixes with the air into an exactly metered, explosive mixture. By the
time the air-fuel mixture reaches the combustion chamber, it is dry.
Liquid gasoline cannot burn.

When the explosive mixture of air and gasoline is compressed 5
tightly, a spark is sent through the mixture, setting it on fire, which
results in the heat and expansion used to push the piston down the

"The Internal Combustion Engine" by Athan Constantin. A previously unpublished work
submitted as a student paper in a class taught by Professor Halsey P. Taylor at California
State Polytechnic University, Pomona, California. Reprinted by permission of the author.

cylinder. The ignition system furnishes a spark to each spark plug when its cylinder is full of the compressed air-fuel mixture. Because the 12 volts of the average car battery are not enough to jump the gap of a spark plug, a transformer, called an ignition coil, is used to step up the battery voltage to about 20,000 volts, which is high enough to jump the spark plug gap with ease.

6    A distributor, driven by the engine in exact time, is an electrical switch which triggers the high voltage impulses and sends them to each spark plug in turn. It is a very exacting task. Its precision can be imagined only when one realizes that the spark must jump the spark plug gap at that precise instant when the piston is close to the top of its cylinder, with the trapped explosive air-fuel mixture compressed and ready to be ignited.

7    To realize the enormity of this exacting task, imagine an 8-cylinder engine operating at 4000 rpm. In 1 minute, the ignition system will have to furnish and deliver 16,000 sparks, each one sent to the proper plug and timed to the split fraction of a second when the piston is close to the end of its compression stroke. This is almost 300 sparks each second!

8    The lubrication system provides a constant flow of filtered oil to all moving parts of the engine. The system consists of an oil pan to store the oil, a pump to circulate it, a filter to remove solid abrasive particles, and an oil gauge or light in the driver's compartment for checking purposes.

9    The operation of this system is very important. Failure of the oil supply will ruin the engine in a very few moments. Fluid lubricants keep metallic parts from rubbing. Should rotating or sliding parts be permitted to come into contact with each other, through failure of the oil supply, the resulting friction would cause heat expansion, binding, and destruction of the entire engine.

10    An internal combustion engine derives its power from burning fuel. Unfortunately, not all of this heat can be used, and, if allowed to remain in the engine, it would soon destroy it. The temperature of the burning air-fuel mixture is about 4500°F. Compare this with the boiling point of water, 212°F., and the melting point of iron, 2500°F. If this unused heat were not removed, the engine would soon melt.

11    Coolant picks up the excess combustion heat as it is circulated through the block and heads by a centrifugal-type pump, delivered

to the radiator where it is cooled, and then returned to the water pump for recirculation. The system operates under an elevated pressure, about 14 psi, and contains a thermostat to prevent coolant circulation when the engine is cold in order to promote rapid warm-up. A by-pass system provides circulation through the cylinder heads and block while the thermostat is closed to ensure equalized block expansion.

## Think about:

1. the writer's use of factual language throughout this article. Do you find any wording that suggests feeling?

2. the organization of the article. Note that in paragraph 2 the writer mentions four requirements of this kind of engine. This paragraph serves as a signal to the reader that Constantin will take up each of these requirements in the body of the article—probably in the order in which they are listed here. As you reread the article, take a pencil and note the paragraph in which each of these requirements is mentioned. Note also any transitional phrases the writer has used to take you from one point to the next. You will observe that after he makes his last point, the writer closes without writing a formal concluding paragraph. Do you think the article needs such a paragraph? Why or why not?

3. the writer's awareness of his **audience.** How can you tell as you read the essay that Constantin had a particular kind of reader (that is, a particular *audience*) in mind? What is that audience? How might the essay have been different if it had been prepared for readers of a different kind—for children or for professional automotive repairmen, for example?

## Write about:

the functioning of a machine or tool with moving parts. Explain not only what happens when the mechanism is working or being used but also—as far as you possibly can—why it happens. Write your explanation for a questioning child or for a person from another culture. The machine or tool need not be as complex as the internal combustion engine. It might be a familiar implement from house, yard, office, shop, or schoolroom. It could be a pencil sharpener, typewriter, power saw, lawnmower (mechanical or powered), windmill, furnace, air conditioning unit, washing machine, toaster, or even an eggbeater. Choose an implement you are at least somewhat familiar with.

## Try out:

observing someone using the tool or operating the machine. Take notes on exactly how the parts move—separately and together. Then try to figure out, if you do not already know, why these parts move as they do—what relationship one movement has to another. You may not understand everything about the functioning of the machine or tool, but you will probably understand enough to answer the questions of a child or of a person who has never used a toaster, a washing machine, or whatever you are writing about. If necessary, check with someone who has special knowledge of the machine or tool.

As far as possible, use Constantin's article as a model for your writing. You can probably use language in the way he does, sticking to facts and leaving yourself and your feelings out of the report altogether. And although your article may be briefer and less complex than Constantin's, you can probably use an organization much like his. That is, early in your paper you can show the reader the several basic operations of the mechanism (as in ¶ 2) and then you can take up each of these basic operations in turn. Probably, for your purpose, one paragraph will be enough for each of these operations.

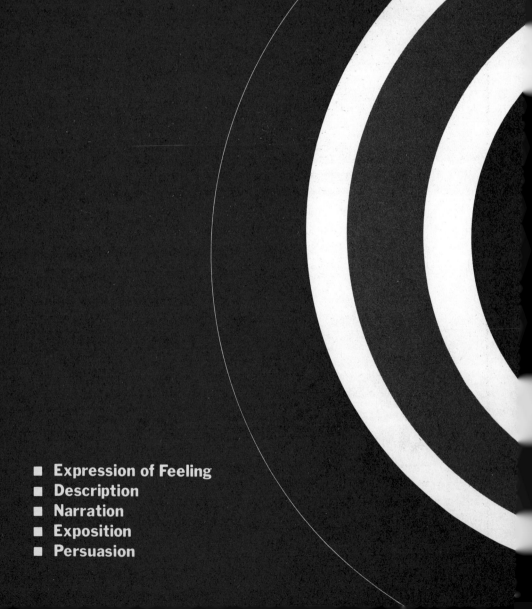

# LEVEL
# THREE

# EXPRESSION OF FEELING

Selection Nineteen

*Bedtime*

## Look for:

1. the picture the poet creates. Where are these people? What objects are mentioned? What time of year is it?

2. the shared feeling the poet describes.

3. these words:
   **drowse (DROWZ)—to be in a sleepy state, not yet asleep** [7]
   **accord (uhk-CORD)—agreement, togetherness** [8]

# Bedtime

**Denise Levertov**

We are a meadow where the bees hum,
mind and body are almost one

as the fire snaps in the stove
and our eyes close,

and mouth to mouth, the covers                    5
pulled over our shoulders,

we drowse as horses drowse afield,
in accord; though the fall cold

surrounds our warm bed, and though
by day we are singular and often lonely.          10

## Think about:

1.  the feeling established by the first line. How does the poet show the reader that these people are comfortable with themselves and with each other?

2.  the relationship between these people. Is this a love poem?

3.  the metaphorical expressions in stanzas 1 and 4. How do these develop the main feeling of the poem? (See pp. 48–49 on *metaphors* and *similes*.)

Denise Levertov, *The Sorrow Dance.* Copyright © 1966 by Denise Levertov. Reprinted by permission of New Directions.

4.  the ending of the poem. Were you surprised when Levertov brought up the idea of loneliness? Why do you suppose she did?

## Write about:

a moment when you realized that you shared a special feeling with another person. The feeling you choose does not have to be a commitment to a lifelong love—although it could be. It might be the satisfaction you felt as you discovered that you and a recent acquaintance were becoming really close friends or the pleasure you experienced as you and a young child or an older person did something special together.

## Try out:

writing a short piece this time (probably one paragraph, beginning with a topic sentence), in which you pay particular attention to *selection of details*. As Levertov does, select a few especially appropriate details that set the scene, establish the atmosphere, and get across the feeling you chose to write about. Note how Levertov's selection of background details—"the fire snaps in the stove," "the covers pulled over our shoulders"—show the reader the peacefulness of the couple at bedtime.

## Selection Twenty

*Winners, Losers, or Just Kids?*

# Look for:

1.  the writer's use of the terms "winners" and "losers." What does he mean by these terms? How appropriate does he think they are as labels for high-school students?

2.  these words:
    **flaunted (FLAWN-t'd)—showed off** [1]

    **metamorphoses (met-ah-MORE-f'-seez)—changes. (You may have studied or heard about the metamorphosis of a butterfly; the change—as it develops in its cocoon—from a crawling larva.)** [4]

    **morose (muh-ROHSS)—glum, depressed, and showing it** [7]

    **flair (FLARE)—talent plus enthusiasm** [7]

    **escapade (ESS-kah-pade)—adventure, especially one that is against the rules** [11]

    **presumptuous (pree-ZUMP-chew-us or pree-ZUMP-shuss)—arrogant, having a know-it-all attitude** [11]

# Winners, Losers, or Just Kids?

Dan Wightman

1    If I envied anyone in high school, it was the winners. You know who I mean. The ones who earned straight A's and scored high on their Scholastic Aptitude Tests. The attractive ones who smiled coyly, drove their own sport cars and flaunted those hard, smooth bodies that they kept tan the year round.

2    By contrast, my high-school friends were mostly losers. We spent a lot of time tuning cars and drinking beer. Our girlfriends were pale and frumpy, and we had more D's than B's on our report cards. After graduation, many of us went into the Army instead of to a university; two of us came back from Vietnam in coffins, three more on stretchers. On weekends, when we drank Colt 45 together in my father's battered Ford, we'd laughingly refer to ourselves as the "out crowd." But, unless we were thoroughly blotto, we never laughed hard when we said it. And I, for one, rarely got blotto when I was 16.

3    The reason I mention this is that last month 183 winners and losers from my Northern California high-school graduating class got together at a swank country club for a revealing 15-year reunion.

4    Predictably, only happy and successful people attended. The strange thing, though, was that the people I once pegged as losers outnumbered the winners at this reunion by a visible margin. And, during a long session at the bar with my informative friend Paula, I got an earful about the messy lives of people I'd once envied, and the remarkable metamorphoses of people I'd once pitied.

5    Paula reported that Len, a former class officer, was now a lost soul in Colorado, hopelessly estranged from his charming wife. Tim, one of the sorriest students I'd ever known, was a successful sportswriter, at ease with himself.

6    Estelle, who was modestly attractive in her teens, was now a

part-time stripper in the Midwest, working to support her young son. Connie, a former car-club "kitten" had become a sophisticated international flight attendant.

Paula told me that Gary, a college scholarship winner, was overweight, underemployed and morose. Ron, who had shown little flair for music, had become a symphony violinist. 7

Sipping a Piña Colada, I thought to myself how terribly mistaken my senior counselor had been when she told me that high-school performance indicates how one will fare later. 8

I looked at Paula, a high-school troublemaker with a naughty smile, whose outgoing personality and rebellious spirit had endeared her to me so long ago. Together, we once stole a teacher's grade book, changed some of our low marks, then dropped the book in the lost-and-found box. The savvy teacher never said a word about the incident, but at the end of the year, when report cards were issued, gave us the D's we deserved. 9

Now Paula was a housewife, a volunteer worker and the mother of two sons. She wore a marriage-encounter pin on her modest dress, and sat at the bar tippling Perrier on ice. 10

She shook her head when I reminded her of the grade-book escapade, and the sheepish look on her face reminded me how presumptuous it is to anticipate the lives of others. 11

It also got me thinking about my own life since high school—how I'd gradually shaken my loser's image, gotten through college, found a decent job, married wisely, and finally realized a speck of my potential. 12

I thought about numerous situations where I could have despaired, regressed, given up—and how I hadn't, though others had —and I wondered why I was different, and had more luck, less guilt. 13

"The past is fiction," wrote William Burroughs. And, although I don't subscribe to that philosophy entirely, the people I admire most today are those who overcome their mistakes, seize second chances and fight to pull themselves together, day after day. 14

Often they're the sort of people who leave high school with blotchy complexions, crummy work habits, fingernails bitten down to the quick. And of course they're bitterly unsure of themselves, and slow to make friends. 15

But they're also the ones who show up transformed at 15-year reunions, and the inference I draw is that the distinction between 16 winners and losers is often slight and seldom crucial—and frequently overrated.

17  In high school, especially, many people are slow getting started. But, finding their stride, they quickly catch up, and in their prime often return to surprise and delight us—their lives so much richer than we'd ever imagined.

## Think about:

1. the way the writer begins this selection. What hints do you find in the first two paragraphs that suggest the main point the writer is going to make?

2. the author's several direct statements of his main idea. What sentence in paragraph 4 plainly introduces this main idea? Where, later in the essay, does he restate it?

3. the support or evidence Wightman gives for his main point. Do you find this evidence convincing? Why or why not?

## Write about:

the contrast between the way a person you knew some time ago used to be and the way that person is today. This person could be your best friend in junior high, or someone you rarely spoke with in high school, or a person you dated a couple of years ago. Or it could even be yourself if you feel you have changed a lot in the last few years or months. Your purpose will be to show the reader in what ways you feel this person's personality, appearance, and behavior have changed. The changes will not necessarily be improvement or worsening. You do not need to make the person appear all "good" or all "bad" either time. You are not writing a "Before and After Using Our Product" ad! Just describe some changes you noticed.

## Try out:

before you write, making two lists. One should be a list of ways this person looked, talked, and acted at the earlier time you are writing about. The other should be the ways this person is different today. Use these lists for details to draw from as you work on your paper. For example, suppose that you had decided to write about a former neighbor whose appearance and habits changed a lot between the time she moved away and the time you ran into her recently in a downtown department store. Your two lists might read something like this:

Earlier Impression
a. kind to animals—kept many stray dogs and cats
b. always at home in the midst of hobbies, projects, repairs, gardening, cub scout, and other volunteer work
c. wore hair long (and its natural dark color), hardly any make-up, casual clothes that took little care: bluejeans, no-iron blouses and skirts, sandals
d. slow-moving, easygoing, rather quiet
e. overweight, and always ready to enjoy good food, especially sweets

Later Impression
a. wore hair short, styled, and blonde (obviously bleached), complete make-up including blue eyelids, and expensive-looking clothing (coordinated from head to foot)
b. moving briskly (in high-heeled shoes)
c. slim
d. (after I recognized her) chatting about her diet and her bookkeeping job in the store. Chief interests seemed to

be her new billing system and her overtime pay. Enthusi-
astic about living alone in apartment nearby with complete maintenance. "No mess, no bother," she told me.
"Only myself to please."

When you write, try using the organization of "Winners,
Losers, or Just Kids" as at least a general model for your
own organization. Review the "Think About" section above.
An organization something like Wightman's will work even
though he is writing about the change in a number of individuals in a group and you are writing about the change in
only one person. You may find, though, that a briefer conclusion than his will work better for your purpose.

# DESCRIPTION

*Laundromat*

## Look for:

1.   the factual description of the laundromat and its furnishings and equipment. Do you picture the place as you read about it here?

2.   descriptions of the people who are in this laundromat.

3.   these words:
   **dour (DOWR—DOW rhymes with how)—gloomy** [1]

   **kaleidoscopic (kuh-lyd-uh-SCOP-ik)—like a kaleido-
      scope, an instrument or toy which makes changing
      patterns and colors. Varied and lively.** [3]

   **jitterbugging (JIT-ter-bug-ing)—dancing in a jumpy way
      popular in the 1940s (note the metaphorical use
      here: the clothes appear to be dancing)** [3]

   **mesmerized (MESS-mer-ized)—hypnotized** [3]

   **scruffiness (SKRUFF-ee-ness)—shabbiness, a dirty and
      worn out condition** [4]

# Laundromat

**Susan Sheehan**

1    It is one-forty-five on a cold, winter-gray Friday afternoon. There are about a dozen people inside the Apthorp Self-Service Laundromat, between Seventy-seventh and Seventy-eighth Streets on the west side of Broadway. The laundromat is a long, narrow room with seventeen Wascomat washing machines—twelve of them the size that takes two quarters, five of them the size that takes three—lined up on one side of the room, and nine dryers on the other. At the back of the alleylike room, four vending machines dispense an assortment of laundry supplies, which cost ten cents an item, to the younger customers; the older customers (more cost-conscious? more farsighted?) bring their own soap powders or liquids from home in small boxes or plastic bottles. On the laundromat's drab painted walls are a clock and a few signs: "No Tintex Allowed," "Last Wash: 10 P.M.," "Not Responsible for Personal Property," "Pack As Full As You Want." On the drab linoleum floor are two trash cans (filled to the brim), a wooden bench, three shabby chairs (occupied), and a table, on which a pretty young black girl is folding clothes, and at which a dour, heavyset black woman in her sixties is eating lunch out of a grease-stained brown paper bag. The heavyset woman has brought no clothes with her to the laundromat. The regular patrons believe she has nowhere else to go that is warm, and accept her presence. On a previous visit, she had tossed a chicken bone at someone, wordlessly, and the gesture had been accepted, too, as a reasonable protest against the miserableness of her life.

2    Half the people in the laundromat have two washing machines going at once. The machines keep them busy inserting coins, stuffing in clothes, and adding detergents, bleaches, and fabric softeners at various stages of the cycle (twenty-five minutes). The newly

From The Talk of the Town, *The New Yorker*, February 20, 1971. Reprinted by permission; © 1971 The New Yorker Magazine, Inc.

washed clothes are retrieved from the washing machines and transferred, in a swooping motion, across the narrow corridor to the dryers. No one dares leave the laundromat to attend to other errands while his clothes are drying (at the rate of ten cents for ten minutes, with most things requiring twenty or thirty minutes), because it is known that clothes that have been left to their own devices in the dryers have disappeared in a matter of five minutes.

A middle-aged man whose clothes are in a small washing machine 3 is standing in front of it reading a sports column in the *News*, but most of the other patrons who are between putting-in and taking-out chores seem to be mesmerized by the kaleidoscopic activity inside the machines. In one washing machine, a few striped sheets and pillowcases are spinning, creating a dizzying optical effect. In another, a lively clothes dance is taking place—three or four white shirts jitterbugging with six or eight pairs of gray socks. In a third, the clothes, temporarily obscured by a flurry of soapsuds, still cast a spell over their owner, who doesn't take her eyes off the round glass window in the front of the machine. The clothes in the dryers—here a few towels, there some men's work pants—seem to be free-falling, like sky divers drifting down to earth. The laundromat smells of a sweet mixture of soap and heat, and is noisy with the hum and whir of the machines. There is little conversation, but a woman suddenly tells her teen-age daughter (why isn't she in school at this hour?) that she takes the family's clothes to the self-service laundromat, rather than to the service laundromat right next door to it, where clothes can be dropped off in the morning and fetched in the evening, because everything at the service laundromat is washed in very hot water, which shrinks clothes that have a tendency to shrink. "Here you're supposed to be able to regulate the temperature of the water, but sometimes I punch the warm button and the water comes out ice-cold," she says. "Oh, well, you sort of have to expect things like that. The owner is very nice. He does the best he can."

A middle-aged man wearing a trenchcoat takes a load of children's 4 clothes out of a large washing machine, folds them neatly, and runs out of the laundromat with the damp pile of girls' school dresses and boys' polo shirts and bluejeans over one arm. (What is his hurry? Will the children's clothes be hung up to dry on a rack at home?) A young Japanese boy, who is holding a book covered with a glossy Columbia University jacket, takes a few clothes out of a dryer. They include a lacy slip and a ruffled pale-pink nightgown with deep-pink rosebuds on it. (His girl's? His bride's? Or only his sister's? Is the nightgown's owner at work, putting him through school, or has she become a Liberated Woman and declined to go to the laundromat?) Two little children run down the narrow center aisle playing tag, chanting in Spanish, tripping over laundry carts, and meeting with scowls from the grownups. A washing machine goes on the blink. Someone goes next door to the service laundromat to summon the proprietor, who comes over immediately, climbs on top of the broken machine, reaches behind it, and restores it to working order in no time. He apologizes, in a Polish accent, to one of his regular customers for the scruffiness of the three chairs on the premises. "Six months ago, I brought in here three first-class chairs," he says. "Fifty-dollar chairs. The next day, they were gone."

5    People come and go, but the population inside the laundromat remains constant at about a dozen. The majority of the customers are blacks and Puerto Ricans who live in nearby tenements and welfare hotels. Most of the whites in the neighborhood live in apartment houses, and have washing machines and dryers in their apartments or in the basements of their buildings, or send their clothes out to local Chinese laundries. One white woman, a blonde in her fifties, says, to no one in particular, that she comes to the laundromat because the laundry room in the basement of her apartment building is not safe. "There have been incidents there," she says meaningfully. "I would love to have my own washing machine, but the landlord says he has to pay for the water, so he won't allow it. I hate coming here and wasting an hour in this depressing place. I wash everything I can by hand at home; that way, I only have to come here with the big things every two weeks, instead of every week. I dream of having my own washing machine and dryer. If I had my own machines, I could fix myself a cup of coffee and a bun, turn on the TV, and sit down in my easy chair; meanwhile, the clothes would all be getting done. It would be heaven."

# Think about:

1. the organization of this description. Why do you suppose the writer starts out with a picture of the physical surroundings and then moves to portraying the people in the place?

2. the writer's *tone,* especially in her comments about the people. Can you imagine how different your view of the people in this laundromat would be if they had been described by a TV comedian? A fashion designer? A social worker? An etiquette advisor? How would you describe Susan Sheehan's **tone,** that is, what is her attitude toward the people she is describing? Is she sarcastic? Angry? Gushy? Sympathetic? Totally neutral?

# Write about:

a public place, describing it somewhat as you did the place you wrote about in the assignment for "The Hamburger Stand" (see p. 27). But this time focus on some of the people in the place whom you find especially interesting or representative of the atmosphere. Tell how they look, what they are doing there, and how they interact with each other —including how they talk to each other. Give just enough factual description of the physical surroundings so that the reader can picture the scene.

# Try out:

first, observing the place and the activities in it carefully. Again, take notes on what you see and hear. But this time try to get down some people's words just as they say them. Note how Sheehan's description becomes especially vivid when she includes dialogue that reveals people's thoughts and feelings. When you write your paper, select some of the quotations and work them into your paragraphs of description to get across the atmosphere of the place (see p. 21 on quotation marks used with *dialogue*). See also ¶¶ 3, 4, and 5 of "Laundromat" for Sheehan's use of quotation marks.

As you write, you can also use Sheehan's article to some extent as a model for organization. That is, you can begin with a brief description of the place and then proceed to create a picture of the people there and the way they relate to each other.

*The Apricot Grove*

# Look for:

1.  the writer's unusual description of a grove of fruit trees in the first sentence of this selection from a fictional work (see p. 29 on *fiction*).

2.  the character's feelings about the grove and what he is doing there. Note that the vivid description throughout this selection is presented from the character's **point of view.** Literally, the "point" or place from which this character views the apricot grove is right in the middle of it, looking constantly into the trees. In addition to this literal point of view, he has a personal or emotional point of view, that is, a particular way of looking at things. What is it?

3.  the kind of language the writer uses in describing the scene. Note that there is more judgment language and less factual language than you found in most of the descriptive works you read earlier in this book. Why does the writer use *judgment language* here? (See p. 24 on *judgment words* and *factual language.*)

4.  these words:
    **respite (RESS-pit)—rest, relief, recess, a break** [1]
    **savor (SAY-v'r)—taste** [1]
    **replenish (ree-PLEN-ish)—put back, refill** [1]
    **follicles (FOLL-lih-kulz)—hollows from which hairs grow** [1]
    **tortilla (tor-TEE-ya)—a kind of unleavened bread made from corn flour (or wheat flour) and patted into a round, thin, flat shape, and used especially in Mexican cooking. A Spanish word.** [3]

# The Apricot Grove

**Raymond Barrio**

1    No matter which way he turned, he was trapped in an endless maze of apricot trees, as though forever, neat rows of them, neatly planted, row after row, just like the blackest bars on the jails of hell. There had to be an end. There had to be. There—trapped. There had to be a way out. Locked. There had to be a respite. Animal. The buckets and the crates kept piling up higher. Brute. He felt alone. Though surrounded by other pickers. Beast. Though he was perspiring heavily, his shirt was powder dry. Savage. The hot dry air. The hot dry air sucking every drop of living moisture from his brute body. Wreck. He stopped and walked to the farthest end of the first row for some water, raised the dented dipper from the brute tank, drank the holy water in great brute gulps so he wouldn't have to savor its tastelessness, letting it spill down his torn shirt to cool his exhausted body, to replenish his brute cells and animal pores and stinking follicles and pig gristle, a truly refined wreck of an animal, pleased to meetcha. Predator.

2    Lunch.

3    Almost too exhausted to eat, he munched his cheese with tortillas, smoked on ashes, then lay back on the cool ground for half an hour. That short rest in the hot shade replenished some of his humor and resolve. He felt his spirit swell out again like a thirsty sponge in water. Then up again. The trees. The branches again. The briarly branches. The scratching leaves. The twigs tearing at his shirt sleeves. The ladder. The rough bark. The endlessly unending piling up of bucket upon box upon crate upon stack upon rack upon mound upon mountain. He picked a mountain of cots automatically. An automator. A beast. A ray of enemy sun penetrated the tree that was hiding him and split his forehead open. His mind whirred. He

blacked out. Luckily he'd been leaning against a heavy branch. His feet hooked to the ladder's rung. His half-filled bucket slipped from his grasp and fell in slow motion, splattering the fruit he'd so laboriously picked. To the ground.

## Think about:

1.   the way Barrio portrays his fictional character. Note especially the one-word sentences—"Animal." "Brute." "Savage."—for example. Whose point of view do these words express? (See p. 120 on *point of view.*) Is Barrio using these words to describe the character? Or is he showing you that the character describes himself this way because of the way he feels he is being treated?

2.   the author's use of incomplete sentences throughout these paragraphs. How does this style of writing communicate the character's emotional and physical state? (See pp. 24 and 29 on the uses of sentence fragments—incomplete sentences—by professional writers.)

## Write about:

an experience you have had in which you were very much aware of your surroundings. As you tell what happened, focus on how things appeared to you and how you felt about them. Note how Barrio focuses on his character's perceptions and feelings. The experience you write about might be one you remember with pleasure, like a long-distance bike ride or a dance or other festive occasion. Or it could be a miserable or frightening experience like getting lost or being physically detained unfairly—or even suffering a bad job experience similar to that of Barrio's character in "The Apricot Grove."

## Try out:

describing your surroundings (at the scene of the experience you are writing about) entirely from your point of view at that time. For example, your cousin's wedding may have seemed especially beautiful to you because at the time you were looking forward to your own marriage. (The same scene, described by the baker who brought the wedding cake, might sound disorganized and ordinary.) You need not explain why you felt as you did—you may not even understand why. Just show the reader the scene as you saw it, not holding back your true feelings and not limiting yourself completely to factual language.

To prepare to write this paper, first jot down the physical details you remember noticing. Then add comments about your reactions to these things. Probably the easiest way to organize this paper will be by telling what you did and saw in chronological order, as Barrio does (see p. 13 on *chronological order*). Do not feel, though, that you have to use a writing style as unusual and startling as his.

# NARRATION

*The Summons*

## Look for:

1.  evidence that helps you guess the age of the girl who is the narrator of this fictional story.

2.  evidence that the boy is at a different stage of emotional development from the girl. Notice how Barrett builds up the *conflict* between the two characters.

3.  the sense of the whole story. This time, try reading straight through—for fun—before studying the vocabulary words. Show yourself that you can understand what's going on throughout the story even though there are many words that may be new to you. You will probably find that you can quickly figure out the meanings of some of these words from their **contexts,** that is, the words and phrases around them. (You will also find here and in other reading that you can often catch on to the meaning of a word by associating it with other words that you do know—see "lustrous" and "deciphered" in the vocabulary list below.)

4.　these words:

**ambled** (AM-bulled)—walked slowly [2]

**opulent** (OP-you-lent)—rich-looking [2]

**lustrous** (LUSS-truss)—shiny. Think of luster, a noun. [2]

**languid** (LAN-gwid)—weak, slow-moving [2]

**suavely** (SWAHV-lee)—in a poised manner, smoothly [9]

**secretary** (SEC-r'-tare-ee)—a kind of desk (as used here) [11]

**deciphered** (dee-SY-ferd)—figured out, decoded. From "cipher" meaning number, figure. [11]

**pristine** (priss-TEEN)—"nice," pure, unused [19]

**non-sequitur** (non-SEC-wit-er)—a statement that doesn't follow logically from the one before it (Latin for "It does not follow") [32]

**miffed** (MIFT)—annoyed, with hurt feelings [32]

**unequivocal** (un-ee-KWIV-uh-c'l)—clear, unarguable [60]

**shamming** (SHAM-ming)—pretending, acting [61]

# The Summons
### B. L. Barrett

The screen door flopped shut behind us with its hollow summer   1
sound. "Mama?" I called, but I knew she wasn't home. Everything
proclaimed it. "Wait a sec," I said, unnecessarily, for Dwayne wasn't
going anywhere. I can see him now, scheming, nibbling his lower lip
with his arms folded on his smooth bare chest and his toes gripping
the rug.

I ambled through the house. The blinds were drawn on all the west   2
windows, in the bathroom the polished basin winked, every room had
that look it has when your mother is gone: dim, orderly, opulent
somehow . . . handsomer than you had known. There were lustrous
strokes from a recent vacuuming on all the rugs, and the beds were
made up smooth as cardboard. "Nobody home," said Dwayne when I
came back. He hadn't moved a muscle. "Maybe she's out back," I
said; "'Scuse me." And he padded after me this time, as far as the
kitchen, where, refolding his arms, he planted himself again, to wait
while I checked the yard from the back porch, with my fingers crossed
for fear of finding her after all, drying her hair in the sun, or hanging
clothes, or coming across the fields from the nearest neighbor. But
there was nothing out there except the summertime. A lizard was
doing pushups on a stone, and a striped towel on the line gave a single
languid flap in a breath of air. That was all.

"Nope," I said, re-entering the kitchen and offering Dwayne a   3
peach from a platterful on the sink.

He didn't notice. His folded arms showed off his biceps, and with   4
lifted head, as if he thought it possible to sniff her whereabouts,
asked, "Where do you suppose she is?"

"I don't know."   5

"When do you think she'll be back?"   6

"To cook dinner."   7

He led the way to the front room and lay down on the sofa, tested   8
the round arm of it for comfort, placed a pillow to his liking, then
lay still and looked at me.

9    I started out fine, like that first day on the pier; as if I were at ease I
stood quiet before him like a finalist in a beauty contest where poise
counted, though in fact it was all I could do not to hop from foot to
foot, as if the rug were hot. But something stupendous seemed to me
at stake, some undefined chance of a lifetime that might be lost by a
nervous movement . . . which indeed there was. Dwayne released me
at last by expressing an admiring hiss through his teeth, and moving
toward the radio I asked suavely, "Want some music?"

10    "Suit yourself," he said, to my surprise getting up. He left the
room and I heard him find the bathroom and go in and shut the
door.

11    When he came back I was sitting at the open secretary leaning
an elbow on the blotter and gazing out the window. The August
fields were visible through the lace panels in the glare of afternoon.
I could smell them, a bricky smell compounded of dried clay and
grasses with the smell of starch and dust in the curtains mixed in.
From the corner of my eye I could see Dwayne settle himself as
before and replace his pillow. The toilet was running and I wished
I had turned the radio on. I deciphered our landlady's name, *Spar-
kenbach,* reversed in dark blue ink here and there on the blotter.
"Will it stop?" Dwayne asked presently.

12    "You have to joggle the handle."

13    He went and joggled the handle and came back with the news we
needed a gismo. "I'll bring one over if I run across one," he offered,
for a third time disposing himself seductively at length on the couch,
this time giving his pillow a punch, while with a fingernail I traced
the landlady's name on the blotter to avoid looking at him. It was
like avoiding looking at a lighted birthday cake in the room with
*Virginia* written on it. "Time's a-wasting," Dwayne said, patting the
sofa edge.

14    I came and sat where he indicated and, hands in lap, gazed at him
with longing.

15    "Now give us a kiss."

16    "I said I'd kiss you back."

17    He shut his eyes and waited.

18    I saw what he was up to: *he* had kissed with no help all summer,
so I could for once . . . And you bet I could have, if I could have
kissed him straight from the way I felt, but the way I felt seemed
out of all proportion to the situation. I could have eaten him with
a spoon, my heart was jumping out of my suit; whereas Dwayne, with
one arm relaxed along his side and the other trailing off the sofa so

his knuckles brushed the rug, appeared so calm. He sat, or rather lay, it seemed to me, in judgment: What kind of kiss did he want? What kind did he expect? What kind would he approve of? That, above all, a girl had to consider.

I placed my hands, as upon the lid of a treasure, on his chest. It 19 felt cool, but his heart was beating in it with an impassioned thump thump thump as stormily as mine. His eyelids barely quivered, a trace of salt from our swim lay in his straight lashes, and such a sigh fetched up in me, I had to clench my teeth to stifle it. Stealthily, I expelled it through my nose, then I leaned from the waist, gave him a briefly lingering pristine peck, and with a mournful conscious-ness of failure sat upright again.

Dwayne pretended he hadn't even felt it and was still waiting. He 20 did not stir or speak.

"Well, what kind of kiss do you want?" I demanded, as if I had 21 been smooching him for a week, every way there was, and come to the end of my resources.

He opened his eyes, studied me a moment, then folding his hands 22 on his stomach asked me, "Florence Hohe had a baby, didn't she?"; and added—for I clammed up, of course—"Everyone knows it."

"The girls don't talk about it." 23

"The guys do." 24

They would, I thought. 25

"Aren't girls curious?" 26

"Are boys?" I countered. 27

"It's all they think about." 28

*That* certainly surprised me: "About girls having babies?" 29

"Well, that's part of it." 30

"Slightly," I said. 31

The conversation was a non sequitur if I ever heard one: we were 32 only kissing, for Pete's sake, and though I enjoyed a good talk about life as much as anyone, it miffed me that Dwayne would fritter away any part of this chance alone with me on talk instead of action. I wanted to kiss, lousy though Dwayne considered me at it; though what he thought he knew about it burned me up, when he had never once not gone off on a tangent folding papers, or some other idiot thing. "The girl doesn't have to have a baby," Dwayne said.

"Baloney," I thought, thinking of Dot's and Leo Jay's incessant 33 worry. I shifted my position so Dwayne wouldn't imagine I couldn't wait to resume the kissing lesson.

34     "She can pick a boy who knows what he's doing."

35     (Ha. Girl quizzes boy: Do you know what you're doing?)

36     "If I was a girl, I'd be curious."

37     "Girls are."

38     ". . . about the Wedding Night," he specified.

39     "You bet."

40     "Waiting till then. Me . . .". He wagged his head and clucked his tongue; "I couldn't do it."

41     "You could. There's plenty of reasons to."

42     "Besides not to get pregnant?"

43     I nodded, shrinking at the word, which was in a category with *buttocks.*

44     "I can't think of any. Except," he amended, noting my silence, "if a person thinks it's wrong, which I don't happen to, do you?"

45     "Heck no. It's nature."

46     "Then I can't think of any."

47     "You could if you were a girl."

48     "Such as."

49     "Well, to name one thing, the first thing . . ."

50     At my reluctance to proceed, Dwayne pursed his lips as if to say, "See? There isn't any."

51     "I've heard it hurts the first time."

52     Astonishment. "Where'd you hear that?"

53     "Never mind."

54     "Phah."

55     "You may say *phah.* Hurts the girl."

56     "If I was that scared, I'd be an old maid."

57     "Not scared," I corrected him firmly. "Just not in a hurry."

58     Dwayne fell silent. He munched his lip awhile, regarding me with speculative eyes, then gently he nudged me to my feet and stood up himself, stretching and yawning.

59     I wanted to scratch his face. I was not aware, it never made my List that he had propositioned me and I had turned him down, but even if I had been, I wouldn't have seen why that should end the kissing. I didn't know yet boys prefer anything to kissing, even with an expert, unless it can lead somewhere, and when next Dwayne lustily bethought him of the peaches he hadn't even looked at when I offered them in the first place, I took it personally, as a clear comment upon my charms, my technique and, most insulting of all, my potential. I really wanted to scratch his face at that, but I

followed him into the kitchen and, side by side, bending over the sink for the juice to drip, we ate peaches as if they were going out of style. We ate the whole platterful. When they were gone we splashed our mouths from the cold faucet and wiped them on our forearms, then, turning, faced each other dripping water from our hands onto the linoleum. In the alcove, the refrigerator with its great coil on top shuddered to life, startling us both, and then Dwayne looking me in the face wiped his hands on me. Not playfully: there was no mistaking it for a joke or teasing. Deliberately and firmly he placed them starting high up under my armpits so I felt their pressure first flattening my breasts at the sides and then slowly down over my waist and hips.

A fearful thrill, like nothing I had ever known or heard of sped  60
through me—an unequivocal sexual summons, like an angry ring at the door. It was the law of life ringing, and high inside me a funny, buzzing trill began, like a rattler's warning.

I yelped and leaped back and, shamming that I thought he was  61
horsing around, wiped my hands on him in return, and under that stroke, Dwayne shut his eyes and I gazed at him appalled; he stood arms at sides, his chin a trifle lifted, solemner than I had ever seen him—ever had seen anyone. "Again," he whispered, and drew a quivering breath just like Leo Jay when Dot butterfly-kissed him.

"Ha ha! You're it!" I cried, pelting him with a peach pit. It struck  62
his chest, he opened his eyes like a wakened sleepwalker, and I lammed out of there.

He didn't chase me, but looking neither to right nor left passed  63
me by (where I was lurking in the dining room anticipating a romp) so offended in his manhood it even showed from the back. He walked straight through the house and out the front door.

## Think about:

1.    the author's use of homely details (the running toilet, the
      sudden noise of the refrigerator turning on) to show the
      reality of the situation. Are these details believable? Do they
      strike you as funny?

2.     the dialogue in the "talk about life." What is Dwayne trying to accomplish with his line of talk? What is Virginia trying to accomplish with hers?

3.     how the scene after Dwayne and Virginia eat the peaches shows that Dwayne is in the mood for serious lovemaking.

4.     the contrast between Dwayne's feelings at that moment and Virginia's. How does she react in trying to deal with his feelings—and hers?

## Write about:

a situation in which you were in *conflict* with another person. This time choose not a physical conflict but, instead, one that involved feelings, goals, or values. The situation might be your rivalry with a friend for a high-school class office or position of athletic leadership. Or it might be a disagreement between you and your boyfriend or girlfriend over long-range plans (for a wedding date? for the location of your future home? for careers for both of you?). Or it could be a conflict between you and an employer or coworker over how to get the job done efficiently or in an ethically acceptable way. Or it might even be a dating scene from your own experience that "The Summons" reminds you of. Again, you will be writing a narrative, as you did in the writing assignments for " 'Surgeon' in a Submarine" (p. 60) and "Old Yeller, the Dog Who Knew When to Fight" (p. 68). But this time, instead of concentrating on fast action, you will be showing how two people contended with each other over a goal, prize, or principle.

## Try out:

using dialogue to show the conflict between two people. Try to make your dialogue as realistic and convincing as possible. Note how genuine Barrett's dialogue seems. For example, in ¶¶ 21 to 57, the verbal exchange leaves no doubt that a real boy and girl could have spoken such lines in an actual life situation. Although you will probably not want to write as much dialogue as appears in this selection, you should include at least a few typical remarks made by the people you are writing about as you tell their story. If you wish, you can give both people fictitious names and write about yourself in the third person, that is, "he, him, his" instead of "I, me, mine."

Again, start your story with direct action. That is, tell where the people are and what's going on, as Barrett does. You might even start your story with a line of dialogue that will point the way to the forthcoming action. (For example, "I won't do it," I said to the dispatcher. "That's one place I'm not driving into after dark to pick up *any* fare.") Then keep the action going throughout your story, *showing* the reader how the conflict developed and how it was settled. The solution to the conflict—that is, how the disagreement ended or how the problem was solved—will be the high point of your story.

---

*Selection Twenty-Four*

---

*Warm River*

## Look for:

1.  the meaning of the title. In this story you can be sure it is especially important because the phrases "the warm river" and "warm water" keep appearing in key places—for example, in the first paragraph and near the end of the story.

2.  the change in the narrator's attitude. What brings it about? Is it convincing?

3.  these words:
    **momentum (mo-MENT-um)—a rate of speed that you keep up as long as you keep moving** [2]
    **pendulum (PEN-d'you-lum)—a heavy weight that swings back and forth, as in a clock** [2]
    **hack (HAK)—taxi** [16]
    **inaudibly (in-AW-d'-blee)—without noise or in a manner so quiet it can't be heard** [39]

# Warm River

### Erskine Caldwell

1    The driver stopped at the suspended footbridge and pointed out to me the house across the river. I paid him the quarter fare for the ride from the station two miles away and stepped from the car. After he had gone I was alone with the chill night and the star-pointed lights twinkling in the valley and the broad green river flowing warm below me. All around me the mountains rose like black clouds in the night, and only by looking straight heavenward could I see anything of the dim afterglow of sunset.

2    The creaking footbridge swayed with the rhythm of my stride and the momentum of its swing soon overcame my pace. Only by walking faster and faster could I cling to the pendulum as it swung in its wide arc over the river. When at last I could see the other side, where the mountain came down abruptly and slid under the warm water, I gripped my handbag tighter and ran with all my might.

3    Even then, even after my feet had crunched upon the gravel path, I was afraid. I knew that by day I might walk the bridge without fear; but at night, in a strange country, with dark mountains towering all around me and a broad green river flowing beneath me, I could not keep my hands from trembling and my heart from pounding against my chest.

4    I found the house easily, and laughed at myself for having run from the river. The house was the first one to come upon after leaving the footbridge, and even if I should have missed it, Gretchen would have called me. She was there on the steps of the porch waiting for me. When I heard her familiar voice calling my name, I was ashamed of myself for having been frightened by the mountains and the broad river flowing below.

5    She ran down the gravel path to meet me.

"Did the footbridge frighten you, Richard?" she asked excitedly, 6
holding my arm with both of her hands and guiding me up the path
to the house.

"I think it did, Gretchen," I said; "but I hope I outran it." 7

"Everyone tries to do that at first, but after going over it once, 8
it's like walking a tightrope. I used to walk tightropes when I was
small—didn't you do that, too, Richard? We had a rope stretched
across the floor of our barn to practice on."

"I did, too, but it's been so long ago I've forgotten how to do it 9
now."

We reached the steps and went up to the porch. Gretchen took 10
me to the door. Someone inside the house was bringing a lamp into
the hall, and with the coming of the light I saw Gretchen's two
sisters standing just inside the open door.

"This is my little sister, Anne," Gretchen said. "And this is 11
Mary."

I spoke to them in the semidarkness, and we went on into the hall. 12
Gretchen's father was standing beside a table holding the lamp a
little to one side so that he could see my face. I had not met him
before.

"This is my father," Gretchen said. "He was afraid you wouldn't 13
be able to find our house in the dark."

"I wanted to bring a light down to the bridge and meet you, but 14
Gretchen said you would get here without any trouble. Did you get
lost? I could have brought a lantern down with no trouble at all."

I shook hands with him and told him how easily I had found the 15
place.

"The hack driver pointed out to me the house from the other side 16
of the river, and I never once took my eyes from the light. If I had
lost sight of the light, I'd probably be stumbling around somewhere
now in the dark down there getting ready to fall into the water."

He laughed at me for being afraid of the river. 17

"You wouldn't have minded it. The river is warm. Even in winter, 18
when there is ice and snow underfoot, the river is as warm as a
comfortable room. All of us here love the water down there."

"No, Richard, you wouldn't have fallen in," Gretchen said, laying 19
her hand in mine. "I saw you the moment you got out of the hack,
and if you had gone a step in the wrong direction, I was ready to
run to you."

20    I wished to thank Gretchen for saying that, but already she was going to the stairs to the floor above, and calling me. I went with her, lifting my handbag in front of me. There was a shaded lamp, lighted but turned low, on the table at the end of the upper hall, and she picked it up and went ahead into one of the front rooms.

21    We stood for a moment looking at each other, and silent.

22    "There is fresh water in the pitcher, Richard. If there is anything else you would like to have, please tell me. I tried not to overlook anything."

23    "Don't worry, Gretchen," I told her. "I couldn't wish for anything more. It's enough just to be here with you, anyway. There's nothing else I care for."

24    She looked at me quickly, and then she lowered her eyes. We stood silently for several minutes, while neither of us could think of anything to say. I wanted to tell her how glad I was to be with her, even if it was only for one night, but I knew I could say that to her later. Gretchen knew why I had come.

25    "I'll leave the lamp for you, Richard, and I'll wait downstairs for you on the porch. Come as soon as you are ready."

26    She had left before I could offer to carry the light to the stairhead for her to see the way down. By the time I had picked up the lamp, she was out of sight down the stairs.

27    I walked back into the room and closed the door and bathed my face and hands, scrubbing the train dust with brush and soap. There was a row of hand-embroidered towels on the rack, and I took one and dried my face and hands. After that I combed my hair, and found a fresh handkerchief in the handbag. Then I opened the door and went downstairs to find Gretchen.

28    Her father was on the porch with her. When I walked through the doorway, he got up and gave me a chair between them. Gretchen pulled her chair closer to mine, touching my arm with her hand.

29    "Is this the first time you have been up here in the mountains, Richard?" her father asked me, turning in his chair towards me.

30    "I've never been within a hundred miles of here before, sir. It's a different country up here, but I suppose you would think the same about the coast, wouldn't you?"

31    "Oh, but Father used to live in Norfolk," Gretchen said. "Didn't you, Father?"

32    "I lived there for nearly three years."

There was something else he would say, and both of us waited for 33
him to continue.

"Father is a master mechanic," Gretchen whispered to me. "He 34
works in the railroad shops."

"Yes," he said after a while, "I've lived in many places, but here 35
is where I wish to stay."

My first thought was to ask him why he preferred the mountains 36
to other sections, but suddenly I was aware that both he and
Gretchen were strangely silent. Between them, I sat wondering
about it.

After a while he spoke again, not to me and not to Gretchen, but 37
as though he were speaking to someone else on the porch, a fourth
person whom I had failed to see in the darkness. I waited, tense and
excited, for him to continue.

Gretchen moved her chair a few inches closer to mine, her mo- 38
tions gentle and without sound. The warmth of the river came up
and covered us like a blanket on a chill night.

"After Gretchen and the other two girls lost their mother," he 39
said, almost inaudibly, bending forward over his knees and gazing
out across the broad green river, "after we lost their mother, I
came back to the mountains to live. I couldn't stay in Norfolk,
and I couldn't stand it in Baltimore. This was the only place on
earth where I could find peace. Gretchen remembers her
mother, but neither of you can yet understand how it is with
me. Her mother and I were born here in the mountains, and we
lived here together for almost twenty years. Then after she left
us, I moved away, foolishly believing that I could forget. But I
was wrong. Of course I was wrong. A man can't forget the
mother of his children, even though he knows he will never see
her again."

Gretchen leaned closer to me, and I could not keep my eyes from 40
her darkly framed profile beside me. The river below us made no
sound; but the warmth of its vapor would not let me forget that it
was still there.

Her father had bent farther forward in his chair until his arms 41
were resting on his knees, and he seemed to be trying to see someone
on the other side of the river, high on the mountain top above it.
His eyes strained, and the shaft of light that came through the open
doorway fell upon them and glistened there. Tears fell from his face

like fragments of stars, burning into his quivering hands until they were out of sight.

42    Presently, still in silence, he got up and moved through the doorway. His huge shadow fell upon Gretchen and me as he stood there momentarily before going inside. I turned and looked towards him but, even though he was passing from sight, I could not keep my eyes upon him.

43    Gretchen leaned closer against me, squeezing her fingers into the hollow of my hand and touching my shoulder with her cheeks as though she were trying to wipe something from them. Her father's footsteps grew fainter, and at last we could no longer hear him.

44    Somewhere below us, along the bank of the river, an express train crashed down the valley, creaking and screaming through the night. Occasionally its lights flashed through the openings in the darkness, dancing on the broad green river like polar lights in the north, and the metallic echo of its steel rumbled against the high walls of the mountains.

45    Gretchen clasped her hands tightly over my hand, trembling to her fingertips.

46    "Richard, why did you come to see me?"

47    Her voice was mingled with the screaming metallic echo of the train that now seemed far off.

48    I had expected to find her looking up into my face, but when I turned to her, I saw that she was gazing far down into the valley, down into the warm waters of the river. She knew why I had come, but she did not wish to hear me say why I had.

49    I do not know why I had come to see her, now. I had liked Gretchen, and I had desired her above anyone else I knew. But I could not tell her that I loved her, after having heard her father speak of love. I was sorry I had come, now after having heard him speak of Gretchen's mother as he did. I knew Gretchen would give herself to me, because she loved me; but I had nothing to give her in return. She was beautiful, very beautiful, and I had desired her. That was before. Now, I knew that I could never again think of her as I had come prepared.

50    "Why did you come, Richard?"

51    "Why?"

52    "Yes, Richard; why?"

My eyes closed, and what I felt was the memory of the star- 53
pointed lights twinkling down in the valley and the warmth of the
river flowing below and the caress of her fingers as she touched my
arm.

"Richard, please tell me why you came." 54

"I don't know why I came, Gretchen." 55

"If you only loved me as I love you, Richard, you would know 56
why."

Her fingers trembled in my hand. I knew she loved me. There had 57
been no doubt in my mind from the first. Gretchen loved me.

"Perhaps I should not have come," I said. "I made a mistake, 58
Gretchen. I should have stayed away."

"But you will be here only for tonight, Richard. You are leaving 59
early in the morning. You aren't sorry that you came for just this
short time, are you, Richard?"

"I'm not sorry that I am here, Gretchen, but I should not have 60
come. I didn't know what I was doing. I haven't any right to come
here. People who love each other are the only ones—"

"But you do love me just a little, don't you, Richard? You couldn't 61
possibly love me nearly so much as I love you, but can't you tell me
that you do love me just a little? I'll feel much happier after you have
gone, Richard."

"I don't know," I said, trembling. 62

"Richard, please—" 63

With her hands in mine I held her tightly. Suddenly I felt some- 64
thing coming over me, a thing that stabbed my body with its quickness. It was as if the words her father had uttered were becoming
clear to me. I had not realized before that there was such a love as
he had spoken of. I had believed that men never loved women in
the same way that a woman loved a man, but now I knew there could
be no difference.

We sat silently, holding each other's hands for a long time. It was 65
long past midnight, because the lights in the valley below were being
turned out; but time did not matter.

Gretchen clung softly to me, looking up into my face and laying 66
her cheek against my shoulder. She was as much mine as a woman
ever belongs to a man, but I knew then that I could never force
myself to take advantage of her love, and to go away knowing that
I had not loved her as she loved me. I had not believed any such

thing when I came. I had traveled all that distance to hold her in my arms for a few hours, and then to forget her, perhaps forever.

67     When it was time for us to go into the house, I got up and put my arms around her. She trembled when I touched her, but she clung to me as tightly as I held her, and the hammering of her heart drove into me, stroke after stroke, like an expanding wedge, the spears of her breasts.

68     "Richard, kiss me before you go," she said.

69     She ran to the door, holding it open for me. She picked up the lamp from the table and walked ahead up the stairs to the floor above.

70     At my door she waited until I could light her lamp, and then she handed me mine.

71     "Good night, Gretchen," I said.

72     "Good night, Richard."

73     I turned down the wick of her lamp to keep it from smoking, and then she went across the hall towards her room.

74     "I'll call you in the morning in time for you to catch your train, Richard."

75     "All right, Gretchen. Don't let me oversleep, because it leaves the station at seven-thirty."

76     "I'll wake you in plenty of time, Richard," she said.

77     The door was closed after her, and I turned and went into my room. I shut the door and slowly began to undress. After I had blown out the lamp and had got into bed, I lay tensely awake. I knew I could never go to sleep, and I sat up in bed and smoked cigarette after cigarette, blowing the smoke through the screen at the window. The house was quiet. Occasionally, I thought I heard the sounds of muffled movements in Gretchen's room across the hall, but I was not certain.

78     I could not determine how long a time I had sat there on the edge of the bed, stiff and erect, thinking of Gretchen, when suddenly I found myself jumping to my feet. I opened the door and ran across the hall. Gretchen's door was closed, but I knew it would not be locked, and I turned the knob noiselessly. A slender shaft of light broke through the opening I had made. It was not necessary to open the door wider, because I saw Gretchen only a few steps away, almost within arm's reach of me. I closed my eyes tightly for a moment, thinking of her as I had all during the day's ride up from the coast.

Gretchen had not heard me open her door, and she did not know 79
I was there. Her lamp was burning brightly on the table.

I had not expected to find her awake, and I had thought surely 80
she would be in bed. She knelt on the rug beside her bed, her head
bowed over her arms and her body shaken with sobs.

Gretchen's hair was lying over her shoulders, tied over the top of 81
her head with a pale blue ribbon. Her nightgown was white silk,
hemmed with a delicate lace, and around her neck the collar of lace
was thrown open.

I knew how beautiful she was when I saw her then, even though 82
I had always thought her lovely. I had never seen a girl so beautiful
as Gretchen.

She had not heard me at her door, and she still did not know I 83
was there. She knelt beside her bed, her hands clenched before her,
crying.

When I had first opened the door, I did not know what I was 84
about to do; but now that I had seen her in her room, kneeling in
prayer beside her bed, unaware that I was looking upon her and
hearing her words and sobs, I was certain that I could never care for
anyone else as I did for her. I had not known until then, but in the
revelation of a few seconds I knew that I did love her.

I closed the door softly and went back to my room. There I found 85
a chair and placed it beside the window to wait for the coming of
day. At the window I sat and looked down into the bottom of the
valley where the warm river lay. As my eyes grew more accustomed
to the darkness, I felt as if I were coming closer and closer to it, so
close that I might have reached out and touched the warm water
with my hands.

Later in the night, towards morning, I thought I heard someone 86
in Gretchen's room moving softly over the floor as one who would
go from window to window. Once I was certain I heard someone in
the hall, close to my door.

When the sun rose over the top of the mountain, I got up and 87
dressed. Later, I heard Gretchen leave her room and go downstairs.
I knew she was hurrying to prepare breakfast for me before I left to
get on the train. I waited awhile, and after a quarter of an hour I
heard her coming back up the stairs. She knocked softly on my door,
calling my name several times.

I jerked open the door and faced her. She was so surprised at 88 seeing me there, when she had expected to find me still asleep, that she could not say anything for a moment.

89     "Gretchen," I said, grasping her hands, "don't hurry to get me off—I'm not going back this morning—I don't know what was the matter with me last night—I know now that I love you—"

90     "But, Richard—last night you said—"

91     "I did say last night that I was going back early this morning, Gretchen, but I didn't know what I was talking about. I'm not going back now until you go with me. I'll tell you what I mean as soon as breakfast is over. But first of all I wish you would show me how to get down to the river. I have got to go down there right away and feel the water with my hands."

## Think about:

1.     the sense in which the warm river serves as a *symbol* in this story. A **symbol** is anything that an individual or a group of people thinks of as representing or standing for a particular idea. A public symbol is one that represents the same general idea to large numbers of people (for example, to many Americans the American flag represents their country and their loyalty to it). A private symbol has special meaning to an individual. (Of course, a public symbol may have special meaning for an individual too—a meaning beyond that which it has for the general public.) In this story, what does the river *symbolize* to Gretchen's father? What does it *symbolize* to Richard? That is, what idea does Richard come to associate with the river? Why, at the end of the story, does he say he wants to go down and put his hands into it?

2.     the father's attitude toward his dead wife and the effect of his attitude on Richard.

# Write about:

something that you consider an important symbol in your life. It might be a flag—national, state, or organizational. It might be a religious symbol or other public symbol. Or it might be anything from a small piece of jewelry (a wedding ring, for example) to a large natural object. Perhaps you live near something that has special meaning to you—a mountain peak glimpsed from your window, a historic building, a tree in the backyard where you grew up. Perhaps you own some object that, whenever you look at it or pick it up, causes you to have some special feeling because you associate it with certain experiences (this object might be a musical instrument, a special book, or an article of clothing). The symbol you choose will be something that reminds you of past experience and perhaps also gives you hope for the future.

# Try out:

using an organizational pattern that is different from any you have used in previous writing assignments as well as one that is quite different from Caldwell's. (You will not be writing a narrative this time, even though the reading selection you have just finished is a narrative.) Try beginning with a description of the object or whatever it is that you are treating as a symbol. Use the descriptive method you have learned in earlier assignments in this book, that is, describe the object in considerable detail. Then proceed to show its significance to you by giving examples of ways in which it has played a part. If possible, finish up with a short conclusion that sums up the importance to you of this object that you regard as a symbol.

*I Become a Student*

# Look for:

1.   the meaning of the title. In what sense does the author become a "student"?

2.   the author's implied definition of education. In the first two sentences, he suggests that not many people get an "education" at a university. What does he mean by this?

3.   the way Steffens' attitude toward teachers and other authorities changes during his college years.

4.   these words:

**circumvent (sir-come-VENT)—to go around** [1]

**cinches (SIN-chiz)—things that are easy to do (old-fashioned slang)** [2]

**con (KAHN)—study, examine closely. (There are also several other meanings for this small word, many of them slang. You might like to check it in your dictionary.)** [2]

**irrelative (ear-REL-uh-tiv)—(old-fashioned form of irrelevant)—not related to whatever is going on** [2]

**memorandum (mem-oh-RAN-dum)—a note about something the writer wants to remember or to have others take note of** [3]

**epochs (EPP-ocks)—periods of time in history** [4]

**vanity (VAN-ih-tee)—conceit, an attitude of being overly proud of oneself, especially for one's appearance or social position** [5]

**philosophically (fill-uh-SOFF-ick-'lee)—in the broadest sense, with a love of learning. As used here, with a genuine interest in knowledge for its own sake.** [7]

**profound (pro-FOUND)—deep** [8]

**ethics (ETH-iks)—a system of deciding what is right and wrong and acting on your decisions** [9]

**puberty (PEW-burr-tee)—the stage of development in a human being at which having children becomes possible** [12]

# I Become a Student

Lincoln Steffens

It is possible to get an education at a university. It has been done;   1
not often, but the fact that a proportion, however small, of college
students do get a start in interested, methodical study, proves my
thesis, and the two personal experiences I have to offer illustrate it
and show how to circumvent the faculty, the other students, and the
whole college system of mind-fixing. My method might lose a boy
his degree, but a degree is not worth so much as the capacity and
the drive to learn, and the undergraduate desire for an empty bacca-
laureate is one of the holds the educational system has on students.
Wise students some day will refuse to take degrees, as the best men
(in England, for instance) give, but do not themselves accept, titles.

My method was hit on by accident and some instinct. I special-   2
ized. With several courses prescribed, I concentrated on the one or
two that interested me most, and letting the others go, I worked
intensively on my favorites. In my first two years, for example, I
worked at English and political economy and read philosophy. At
the beginning of my junior year I had several cinches in history. Now
I liked history; I had neglected it partly because I rebelled at the way
it was taught, as positive knowledge unrelated to politics, art, life,
or anything else. The professors gave us chapters out of a few books
to read, con, and be quizzed on. Blessed as I was with a "bad
memory," I could not commit to it anything that I did not understand and intellectually need. The bare record of the story of man,
with names, dates, and irrelative events, bored me. But I had discovered in my readings of literature, philosophy, and political economy
that history had light to throw upon unhistorical questions. So I
proposed in my junior and senior years to specialize in history, taking
all the courses required and those also that I had flunked in. With

this in mind I listened attentively to the first introductory talk of Professor William Cary Jones on American constitutional history. He was a dull lecturer, but I noticed that, after telling us what pages of what books we must be prepared in, he mumbled off some other references "for those that may care to dig deeper."

3    When the rest of the class rushed out into the sunshine, I went up to the professor and, to his surprise, asked for this memorandum. He gave it to me. Up in the library I ran through the required chapters in the two different books, and they differed on several points. Turning to the other authorities, I saw that they disagreed on the same facts and also on others. The librarian, appealed to, helped me search the book-shelves till the library closed, and then I called on Professor Jones for more references. He was astonished, invited me in, and began to approve my industry, which astonished me. I was not trying to be a good boy; I was better than that: I was a curious boy. He lent me a couple of his books, and I went off to my club to read them. They only deepened the mystery, clearing up the historical question, but leaving the answer to be dug for and written.

4    The historians did not know! History was not a science, but a field for research, a field for me, for any young man, to explore, to make discoveries in and write a scientific report about. I was fascinated. As I went on from chapter to chapter, day after day, finding frequently essential differences of opinion and of fact, I saw more and more work to do. In this course, American constitutional history, I hunted far enough to suspect that the Fathers of the Republic who wrote our sacred Constitution of the United States not only did not, but did not want to, establish a democratic government, and I dreamed for a while—as I used as a child to play I was Napoleon or a trapper—I promised myself to write a true history of the making of the American Constitution. I did not do it; that chapter has been done or well begun since by two men: Smith of the University of Washington and Beard (then) of Columbia (afterward forced out, perhaps for this very work). I found other events, men, and epochs waiting for students. In all my other courses, in ancient, in European, and in modern history, the disagreeing authorities carried me back to the need of a fresh search for (or of) the original documents or other clinching testimony. Of course I did well in my classes. The history professors soon knew me as a student and seldom put a

question to me except when the class had flunked it. Then Professor Jones would say, "Well, Steffens, tell them about it."

Fine. But vanity wasn't my ruling passion then. What I had was a quickening sense that I was learning a method of studying history and that every chapter of it, from the beginning of the world to the end, is crying out to be rewritten. There was something for Youth to do; these superior old men had not done anything, finally.

Years afterward I came out of the graft prosecution office in San Francisco with Rudolph Spreckels, the banker and backer of the investigation. We were to go somewhere, quick, in his car, and we couldn't. The chauffeur was trying to repair something wrong. Mr. Spreckels smiled; he looked closely at the defective part, and to my silent, wondering inquiry he answered: "Always, when I see something badly done or not done at all, I see an opportunity to make a fortune. I never kick at bad work by my class: there's lots of it and we suffer from it. But our failures and neglects are chances for the young fellows coming along and looking for work."

Nothing is done. Everything in the world remains to be done or done over. "The greatest picture is not yet painted, the greatest play isn't written (not even by Shakespeare), the greatest poem is unsung. There isn't in all the world a perfect railroad, nor a good government, nor a sound law." Physics, mathematics, and especially the most advanced and exact of the sciences, are being fundamentally revised. Chemistry is just becoming a science; psychology, economics, and sociology are awaiting a Darwin, whose work in turn is awaiting an Einstein. If the rah-rah boys in our colleges could be told this, they might not all be such specialists in football, petting parties, and unearned degrees. They are not told it, however; they are told to learn what is known. This is nothing, philosophically speaking.

Somehow or other in my later years at Berkeley, two professors, Moses and Howison, representing opposite schools of thought, got into a controversy, probably about their classes. They brought together in the house of one of them a few of their picked students, with the evident intention of letting us show in conversation how much or how little we had understood of their respective teachings. I don't remember just what the subject was that they threw into the ring, but we wrestled with it till the professors could stand it no longer. Then they broke in, and while we sat silent and highly entertained, they went at each other hard and fast and long. It was after midnight when, the debate over, we went home. I asked the other fellows what they had got out of it, and their answers showed that they had seen nothing but a fine, fair fight. When I laughed, they asked me what I, the D.S., had seen that was so much more profound.

9     I said that I had seen two highly-trained, well-educated Masters of Arts and Doctors of Philosophy disagreeing upon every essential point of thought and knowledge. They had all there was of the sciences; and yet they could not find any knowledge upon which they could base an acceptable conclusion. They had no test of knowledge; they didn't know what is and what is not. And they have no test of right and wrong; they have no basis for even an ethics.

10     Well, and what of it? They asked me that, and that I did not answer. I was stunned by the discovery that it was philosophically true, in a most literal sense, that nothing is known; that it is precisely the foundation that is lacking for science; that all we call knowledge rested upon assumptions which the scientists did not all accept; and that, likewise, there is no scientific reason for saying, for example, that stealing is wrong. In brief: there was no scientific basis for an ethics. No wonder men said one thing and did another; no wonder they could settle nothing either in life or in the academies.

11     I could hardly believe this. Maybe these professors, whom I greatly respected, did not know it all. I read the books over again with a fresh eye, with a real interest, and I could see that, as in history, so in other branches of knowledge, everything was in the air. And I was glad of it. Rebel though I was, I had got the religion of scholarship and science; I was in awe of the authorities in the academic world. It was a release to feel my worship cool and pass. But I could not be sure. I must go elsewhere, see and hear other professors, men these California professors quoted and looked up to as their high priests. I decided to go as a student to Europe when I was through Berkeley, and I would start with the German universities.

12     My father listened to my plan, and he was disappointed. He had hoped I would succeed him in his business; it was for that that he was staying in it. When I said that, whatever I might do, I would never go into business, he said, rather sadly, that he would sell out his interest and retire. And he did soon after our talk. But he wanted me to stay home and, to keep me, offered to buy an interest in a

certain San Francisco daily paper. He had evidently had this in mind for some time. I had always done some writing, verse at the poetical age of puberty, then a novel which my mother alone treasured. Journalism was the business for a boy who liked to write, he thought, and he said I had often spoken of a newspaper as my ambition. No doubt I had in the intervals between my campaigns as Napoleon. But no more. I was now going to be a scientist, a philosopher. He sighed; he thought it over, and with the approval of my mother, who was for every sort of education, he gave his consent.

## Think about:

1.  the writer's main idea. Where in this selection is it stated directly?

2.  what ability Steffens tried to develop in himself instead of a good memory. Why did he do this?

3.  the way Steffens began to make use of the knowledge of the history teacher who was a "dull lecturer" (¶ 2).

4.  the meaning of the author's statement, "history was not a science." Why did this idea excite him so much? What did he think he would do about it?

5.  what Steffens had in mind when he decided to write a "true history" of the Constitution of the United States. What idea was he interested in communicating?

6.  Steffens' method of studying history. In ¶ 5, he says, "I was learning a method of studying history, and . . . every chapter of it . . . is crying out to be rewritten." What would he put in his version that he found distorted or missing in accounts written by "these superior old men"?

7.     Steffens' statement, "I was not trying to be a good boy; I was better than that: I was a curious boy." What do you think he means by the terms "good boy" and "curious boy"? Do you agree with the author that a person who is "curious" makes a better student than one who is "good"? Why or why not?

## Write about:

a learning experience you have had in school (or out of school, if you prefer) that you found either very thought-provoking and rewarding or very frustrating and disappointing. The experience could be with one particular course or it could be (as Steffens' is) with a *kind* of course—English, history, shop, for example. Be sure, though, that you get beyond the level of personalities; for instance, do not criticize a course simply on the ground that you did not like the instructor. Try to do as Steffens does: consider the purpose of what you were trying to find out, and show how successful you were in learning something about it. Note also that Steffens' essay is in part a criticism of the system but primarily a comment on what he learned to do to get beyond the system. Perhaps you want to take this approach in your essay.

## Try out:

using Steffens' method of developing an idea about an educational experience. That is, begin with an introductory paragraph that states directly in a general way the point you are making about your work in a particular course or group of courses. Note that Steffens' second sentence serves as an indirect statement of his main idea. Then proceed, as Steffens does, to recount incidents that illustrate your point, by telling what happened in the classroom or what you did that made this learning experience a success or failure for you. As you relate these incidents, you may want to comment on their importance (as Steffens does in ¶¶ 10 and 11). You may be able to conclude as Steffens does by showing what you decided to do in the future as a result of this experience. (Did you decide to study electronics to qualify for a particular kind of job? Start over again to try to understand math by taking a review course by correspondence? Begin to keep a daily journal as a way of improving your written communication?)

You used an approach very much like this when you wrote the assignment for "The Most Important Day." There you learned to begin a *narrative* with an introductory paragraph stating the thesis, following through with a body paragraph that tells the story, and ending up with a brief concluding paragraph. Here you will be doing the same thing except that you will probably have more than one body paragraph because you will be writing about more than one incident. Furthermore, this time you may want to interrupt your storytelling to comment on the significance of what happened (as Steffens does in ¶¶ 4, 5, 10, and 11).

# EXPOSITION

*As a Horse Sees It*

## Look for:

1.     the author's step-by-step account of the way an Indian trains a wild horse.

2.     what the wild horse is afraid of. How does the trainer get the horse to overcome that fear?

3.     these words:
       **arduous (AR-d'you-us)—hard, strenuous** [1]

       **maneuvers (man-OO-verz)—manipulates, causes to move or act. (You may already know what is meant by the term "military maneuvers.")** [4]

       **rationality (rash-un-AL-ih-tee)—ability to learn** [12]

# As a Horse Sees It

### Chief Buffalo Child Long Lance

The next day our braves began the arduous task of breaking the  1
wild horses to the halter. They used the Indian method, which is
very simple and methodical. While four men held on to a stout
rawhide rope which was noosed around the animal's neck, another
man would approach the horse's head gradually, "talking horse" to
him and making many queer motions and sounds as he went nearer.

"Horse talk" is a low grunt which seems to charm a horse and  2
make him stand perfectly still for a moment or so at a time. It sounds
like "Hoh-hoh," uttered deep down in one's chest. The horse will
stop his rough antics and strain motionless on the rope for a few
seconds; while he is doing this and looking straight at the approaching figure, the man will wave a blanket at him and hiss at him—
*"Shuh! Shuh!"* It takes about fifteen minutes of this to make the
horse realize that the man is harmless, that no motion which he
makes, no sound that he utters, will harm him in any way.

It is a strange fact that a wild horse, of either the ranch or the  3
open ranges, will not react to quiet kindliness at first. He must first
be treated gruffly—but not harshly—and then when he is on a
touching acquaintance with man, kindness is the quickest way to win
his affections.

When the man has reached the head of the horse, his hardest job  4
is to give him the first touch of man's hand, of which the horse seems
to have a deathly fear. He maneuvers for several minutes before he
gets a finger on the struggling nose, and rubs it and allows the horse
to get his smell or scent. When this has been done, the brave loops
a long, narrow string of rawhide around the horse's nose and then
carries it up behind his ears and brings it down on the other side and
slips it under the other side of the nose loop, making something like

a loose-knotted halter, which will tighten up on the slightest pull from the horse.

5    This string is no stronger than a shoe-lace, yet, once the warrior has put it on the horse's head, he tells the other men to let go the strong rawhide thong, and from then on he alone handles the horse with the small piece of string held lightly in one hand. The secret of this is that whenever the horse makes pull on the string, it grips certain nerves around the nose and back of the ears, and this either stuns him or hurts him so badly that he doesn't try to pull again.

6    With the horse held thus, the warrior now stands in front of him and strokes the front of his face and hisses at him at close range. It is the same noise that a person makes to drive away chickens— *"shuh, shuh"*—and perhaps the last sound an untrained person would venture to use in taming a wild, ferocious horse; yet it is the quickest way of gaining a horse's confidence and teaching him not to be afraid.

7    When the warrior has run his fingers over every inch of the horse's head and neck, he now starts to approach his shoulders and flanks with his fingers. The horse will start to jump about again at this, but a couple of sharp jerks on the string stop him, and as he stands trembling with fear, the warrior slowly runs his hand over his left side. When this is finished he stands back and takes a blanket and strikes all of the portions of his body that he has touched and shouts *"Shuh!"* with each short stroke of the blanket.

8    When he has repeated these two operations on the other side of the horse, he now starts to do his legs. Each leg, beginning with his left front leg, must be gone over by his hand, with not an inch of its surface escaping his touch. This is the most ticklish part of the work, for the feet are the horse's most deadly weapons. But two more jerks on the string quiet the horse's resentment, and within another fifteen minutes every square inch of the horse's body has been touched and rubbed, even down to his tail and the ticklish portions of his belly and between his legs.

9    Now the job of breaking the horse is all but finished. There is just one thing to do, and that is to accustom the horse to a man hopping on his back and riding him. This is done very simply, and within about five minutes.

10    The warrior takes the blanket and strikes the horse's back a number of blows. Then he lays the blanket on his back very gently. The

horse will at first buck it off, but another jerk on the string, and he is quieted. The warrior picks the blanket up and lays it across his back again. The horse jumps out from under it perhaps twice before he will stand still. When he has been brought to this point, the man throws the blanket down and walks slowly to the side of the horse and presses down lightly. He keeps pressing a little harder and harder, until finally he places his elbows across his back and draws his body an inch off the ground, putting his full weight on the back of the animal. A horse might jump a little at the first experience of this weight, but he will stand still the next time it is tried.

After the warrior has hung on his back by his elbows for several 11 periods of about thirty seconds each, he will now very gradually pull himself up, up, up until he is ready to throw his right foot over to the other side. It is a strange fact that few horses broken in this manner ever try to buck. He will stand perfectly still, and the man will sit there and stroke him for a moment and then gently urge him to go, and the horse will awkwardly trot off in a mild, aimless amble, first this way and that—so bewildered and uncertain in his gait that one would think it was the first time he had ever tried to walk on his own feet.

The reason a horse can be broken in the above manner is that he 12 is a remarkably intelligent being with rationality. A chicken has no reason; therefore it goes through its life running away from "shuhs" that will never harm it. This keeps it from getting many extra crumbs that it could leisurely eat if it only had the reason to learn from experience as the horse does.

## Think about:

1.  the author's purpose in this selection, that is, what is he communicating to what audience? Is he writing for people who need instruction in training horses? You probably no-

ticed that Long Lance does not give direct advice to his readers but does give detailed information. What purpose does his narrative or storytelling form suggest?

2. what attitude—or "philosophy of life"—does the author seem to you to suggest in his explanation of how Indians deal with animals?

## Write about:

a process something like the one you just read about—training a wild horse. Choose a process you are familiar with or at least have observed closely. Tell how a skilled or professional worker goes about doing a specific task—shearing a sheep, photographing a young child, styling someone's hair, or teaching people to perform a dance, a gymnastic exercise, or the basic strokes of golf or tennis.

## Try out:

first, observing someone performing this task—even if you have observed it many times before and have done it yourself. Take notes on exactly what is done, step by step.

Then, when you write you will probably find that each step you tell about will fit into a separate paragraph. The first sentence of each paragraph will probably introduce a step and will therefore serve as a topic sentence. But try to avoid repeating the same kind of introductory sentence in each paragraph (for example: "The next step was . . ."). Some of Long Lance's introductory phrases can serve as models for your writing. Note, for instance, "The next day" (¶ 1), "When the man has reached the head of the horse" (¶ 4), "With the horse held thus" (¶ 6), and "Now the job of breaking the horse is all but finished" (¶ 9).

This method of organization and development is very similar to the one you used in the writing assignment for "Get

Out on a Limb" (p. 80). In fact, it is a good idea to read over the instructions for that assignment before you do this one. In this paper, too, you will want to have an attention-getting introductory paragraph and a brief "pulling together" concluding paragraph as well as body paragraphs that give a step-by-step explanation of the process. (The first paragraph of "As a Horse Sees It" will not work as a model for your introduction because this selection is extracted from the middle of a chapter from a longer work and therefore begins more abruptly than you will want to. The last paragraph, however, illustrates one effective way of winding up this kind of report.)

---

*Selection Twenty-Seven*

*Staying Alive*

# Look for:

1.   specific advice the poet gives the reader on surviving in the wilderness.

2.   these words:
   **fire-bow (FYR-boh)—a curved stick to rub against another stick for the purpose of starting a fire** [20]
   **uncanny (un-CAN-nee)—unknowable, mysterious** [55]
   **burrow (BURR-roh)—dig** [83]

# Staying Alive

### David Wagoner

Staying alive in the woods is a matter of calming down
At first and deciding whether to wait for rescue,
Trusting to others,
Or simply to start walking and walking in one direction
5  Till you come out—or something happens to stop you.
By far the safer choice
Is to settle down where you are, and try to make a living
Off the land, camping near water, away from shadows.
Eat no white berries;
10  Spit out all bitterness. Shooting at anything
Means hiking further and further every day
To hunt survivors;
It may be best to learn what you have to learn without a gun,
Not killing but watching birds and animals go
15  In and out of shelter
At will. Following their example, build for a whole season:
Facing across the wind in your lean-to,
You may feel wilder,
But nothing, not even you, will have to stay in hiding.
20  If you have no matches, a stick and a fire-bow
Will keep you warmer,
Or the crystal of your watch, filled with water, held up to
    the sun
Will do the same in time. In case of snow
Drifting toward winter,
25  Don't try to stay awake through the night, afraid of freez-
    ing—
The bottom of your mind knows all about zero;
It will turn you over

And shake you till you waken. If you have trouble sleeping
Even in the best of weather, jumping to follow
With eyes strained to their corners                                30
The unidentifiable noises of the night and feeling
Bears and packs of wolves nuzzling your elbow,
Remember the trappers
Who treated them indifferently and were left alone.
If you hurt yourself, no one will comfort you                      35
Or take your temperature,
So stumbling, wading, and climbing are as dangerous as
    flying.
But if you decide, at last, you must break through
In spite of all danger,
Think of yourself by time and not by distance, counting           40
Wherever you're going by how long it takes you;
No other measure
Will bring you safe to nightfall. Follow no streams: they run
Under the ground or fall into wilder country.
Remember the stars                                                45
And moss when your mind runs into circles. If it should rain
Or the fog should roll the horizon in around you,
Hold still for hours
Or days if you must, or weeks, for seeing is believing
In the wilderness. And if you find a pathway,                     50
Wheel-rut, or fence-wire,
Retrace it left or right: someone knew where he was going
Once upon a time, and you can follow
Hopefully, somewhere,
Just in case. There may even come, on some uncanny eve-           55
    ning,
A time when you're warm and dry, well fed, not thirsty,
Uninjured, without fear,
When nothing, either good or bad, is happening.
This is called staying alive. It's temporary.
What occurs after                                                 60
Is doubtful. You must always be ready for something to come
    bursting
Through the far edge of a clearing, running toward you,
Grinning from ear to ear

And hoarse with welcome. Or something crossing and hover-
   ing
65   Overhead, as light as air, like a break in the sky,
Wondering what you are.
Here you are face to face with the problem of recognition.
Having no time to make smoke, too much to say,
You should have a mirror
70   With a tiny hole in the back for better aiming, for reflecting
Whatever disaster you can think of, to show
The way you suffer.
These body signals have universal meaning: If you are lying
Flat on your back with arms outstretched behind you,
75   You say you require
Emergency treatment; if you are standing erect and holding
Arms horizontal, you mean you are not ready;
If you hold them over
Your head, you want to be picked up. Three of anything
80   Is a sign of distress. Afterward, if you see
No ropes, no ladders,
No maps or messages falling, no searchlights or trails blazing,
Then, chances are, you should be prepared to burrow
Deep for a deep winter.


## Think about:

1.   some of the specific pieces of advice the poem gives for
     survival in the wilderness. List the directions you remem-
     ber that you consider important. Which of these are dif-
     ferent from the rules you would have expected to follow?
     Are you convinced that the poet's directions make sense?
     Why or why not?

2.   the way the poet words his advice on wilderness survival.
     Note that the language used is for the most part literal

rather than metaphorical—for example, "camping near water," "eat no white berries" (see p. 48 on *metaphor*). But even where the directions sound as literal as a motor vehicles' department handbook, notice that the reader is encouraged to make **inferences** that go beyond the directly stated meanings. That is, readers are expected to reason out intended meanings from information they have been given earlier in the poem and from their own experience. What inferences about wilderness survival can you draw from each of the following?

lines 7–8: make a living off the land
(Does this phrase mean here what it usually means—planting, growing, harvesting?)
line 8: camping . . . away from shadows
(Why should you avoid shadows?)
lines 14–16: watching birds and animals go . . . At will
(What can you learn from them?)
line 17: Facing across the wind in your lean-to
(Why?)
line 25: Don't try to stay awake through the night
(Why shouldn't you? And why don't you need to?)
lines 49–50: seeing is believing in the wilderness
(Why is your sense of sight so important when you are lost in the wilderness?)
lines 83–84: be prepared to burrow/Deep for a deep winter
(How can a human "burrow deep"? An animal may do it by digging a hole in the ground. How could a person make a place to stay warm and comfortable in the winter woods?)

3. the significance of the title. Why do you suppose Wagoner called the poem "Staying Alive" rather than "Staying Alive in the Wilderness"? What can you *infer* from (that is, make a reasoned guess about) his advice about survival in the wilderness that would apply to survival anywhere—when a person is lost (or confused or ignored)? Choose two or three of the lines quoted in *Think about #2* and tell how you could use this advice for living safely in a crowded city, on a college campus, or in some other nonwilderness environment.

## Write about:

how to survive—or get along—in a particular place and/or situation, giving specific and thoughtful advice that would be useful to someone younger or less experienced in that situation. You may choose something relatively trivial such as how to "survive" a blind date, or you may choose a serious but not dangerous situation such as how to "get into" studying your first quarter at college. But do pay particular attention to organizing your information so that a reader could follow your advice.

## Try out:

having in mind a specific reader as your audience—perhaps a younger brother or sister or a good friend or even an older relative. Try putting your advice in the form of a letter to this person. Although the letter form is more informal than the forms you have been using for previous assignments, nevertheless a well-written letter has some kind of structure. For this letter, you will probably have separate paragraphs for each major piece of advice you give, with a topic sentence for each. And you will want an introductory paragraph that establishes contact with the reader and tells him or her why you are writing this letter. You will probably find it helpful, before you begin writing, to outline the main points you are going to make.

*Selection Twenty-Eight*

*Everybody Loves an Octopus*

# Look for:

1. the implications of the title. Do you think that everybody loves an octopus? If not, why not?

2. the writer's descriptive account of the usual behavior of octopuses. In what ways is their behavior different from what most people expect of them?

3. several basic characteristics of octopuses the writer stresses.

4. information Pratt-Johnson gives about the wide variety of octopus life and the various conditions in which octopuses live.

5.    these words:

writhing (RYE-thing—with "th" as in "these and those")
—wriggling, squirming, struggling [2]

random (RAN-d'm)—by chance, as happens, without
plan [6]

prey (PRAY)—living creature attacked for use as food
[6]

salivary glands (SAL-ih-vaa-ree)—the glands that pro-
duce saliva (commonly called spit) [7]

exotic (ex-OTT-ik)—unfamiliar, in an exciting or glamor-
ous way [8]

tinged (TINJD)—touched, as with a bit of color from a
paintbrush [8]

retaliate (ree-TAL-ee-ate)—fight back [9]

predator (PRED-uh-tor)—creature that hunts for other
creatures as food [10]

mollusk (MOLL-usk)—shellfish [11]

embryologist (em-bree-OLL-uh-jist)—a specialist in the
study of creatures before birth [17]

cytologist (sy-TAHL-uh-jist)—a specialist in the study of
cells [17]

aerate (A-uhr-ate or AYR-ate)—give air to [20]

# Everybody Loves an Octopus

**Betty Pratt-Johnson**

Everybody loves an octopus . . . except another octopus, maybe 1
—for octopuses like to be alone. "In captivity you can't keep two
together in a tank," says Gil Hewlett, Vancouver Public Aquarium
curator. "Octopuses have their own territory. They're always solitary
except at mating time."

And four Vancouver divers found this to be true on the day of 2
the most exciting hunt of their lives when they caught three enor-
mous octopuses: one was alone, the other two were mating. They
brought all three writhing, eight-armed specimens of *Octopus dof-
leini,* powerful but delicate giants of 60, 70 and 75 pounds, to the
aquarium alive.

This north Pacific species is considered the largest in the world. 3
The arm spread of a fully grown animal may be 32 feet. However,
the octopus is not the fearsome monster most people think it is. It
is one of the most misunderstood creatures in the animal kingdom.

Larry Hewitt, a diver who once wrestled huge Puget Sound oc- 4
topuses for fun and food says: "When faced with a fight-or-run
situation, they run!" Or, the octopus may latch onto the closest hard
object. If you are trying to catch it, that object is you. An experienced wrestler places the octopus against his chest and in most
cases the animal will ride contentedly to the surface in this friendly
hug. To get rid of it, you just pat, stroke or tickle it.

Octopuses are found in nearly all coastal seas. There are about 150 5
known species, ranging from the giants of the Pacific northwest to
the midgets (only a few inches long) in the South China Sea. Most
octopuses are middle-sized and grow to about three or four feet
across. Some sun themselves in the shallows. Others may live as
much as a mile deep or on the ocean floor.

Reprinted, with modification, from January/February 1978 *Oceans,* a publication of the
Oceanic Society 1978. Copyright 1978, 1980 by Betty Pratt-Johnson. Reprinted by
permission. Betty Pratt-Johnson is author of *147 Dives in the Protected Waters of
Washington and British Columbia.*

6    They eat shellfish such as crabs, clams, lobsters, or abalones. Occasionally they catch a fish. Some species such as the "day octopus" in Hawaii hunt by daylight. But most are shy and lie in wait for random prey or hunt at night.

7    An octopus grabs its food with the circular suckers on one or more of its eight strong arms. Depending on the species, there may be as many as 240 suckers in a double row along the length of each arm; they vary from the size of a pinpoint up to 2½ inches in diameter. A quarter-inch sucker requires a pull of six ounces to break its hold. Multiply this by the 2,000 or so suckers found on most common octopuses—even a small one—and it equals considerable pulling force. With these powerful suckers the octopus carries its prey to its mouth and bites it with its beak (an 18-inch octopus has a beak like a parakeet's). Then it secretes poison from its salivary glands to stun or kill the prey. Some octopuses drill holes through clam shells with their long, thin saw-like tongues in order to reach the flesh. Then they use this tongue to scrape out any remaining particles. An octopus can consume its favorite shellfish, the crab, in thirty minutes.

8    Common octopuses have some exotic eating habits too. They are territorial—to the point of being cannibalistic—and will devour an intruder that dares to crowd their space. There have been rare cases of octopuses starting to eat themselves just prior to death. Yet most of their reported contacts with people—even in the wilds—are either friendly or tinged with fear on the part of the octopus.

9    Reports of octopuses biting are rare. Jock MacLean, a retired British Columbia diver who has caught as much as 1,000 pounds of octopus in a day to sell as bait, asserts that it is impossible to make the north Pacific giant bite. He says octopuses always refuse to retaliate.

10    If a frightened octopus will not attack a diver, it will do various other things to save itself. In open water it will flee. Or, protected by one of the speediest color-changing systems in the animal kingdom, it may turn white with fright, or red with rage to alarm its enemy. It can turn greeny-white or brown or reddish-brown, or speckled to disguise itself. You can truly read an octopus's emotions by the color of its face! The skin of a disturbed octopus may become pebbly and push up over the eyes into points resembling horns, which may account for the nickname "devilfish." Sometimes it

squirts sepia, or ink, to distract a predator and numb its sense of smell. Then the octopus will try to escape to hide in its den in the rocks. The Hawaiian word for octopus is *he'e* (pronounced hey-ey) meaning to flee, or flow away, and describes the response of frightened octopuses the world over.

An octopus always looks for a cave or crevice or some enclosure 11 to contain it, almost as if it were trying to find a protective shell like those of most other mollusks, trying to replace the armored casing its own ancestors once wore. "Knowing these habits," says Marcelo de Sousa Vasconcelos of the aquarium in Lisbon, "Portuguese fishermen use a series of attached empty pots for catching octopuses. When they pull up the pots, the octopuses will cling inside and as a rule will not leave their new-found shelter." And the cooking pot is the next home for this loner of the seas!

Though octopuses prefer solitude in the wilds, in captivity they 12 become tame and affectionate, according to Gil Hewlett. "They like to be stroked. They are quite intelligent. And they may play jokes too. Once we had an octopus with a habit of squirting passersby. However, octopuses' curiosity and intelligence sometimes work against them. For example, we had an octopus that pulled the plug in the night and died after the water drained from its tank.

"Then one morning while making rounds we discovered a more 13 mysterious casualty," Hewlett continued. "The foot-long skilfish had been half-eaten, and nothing else was in the tank with it. The next day we caught the octopus red-handed climbing into the skilfish tank to eat the rest of its meal." Hewlett explained that the tanks must be sealed tightly with fine screening at the top because a 60-pound octopus can creep through a hole two inches in diameter. "You must weight down the cover of the tank too," he added "or an octopus will cleverly find how to push it up and escape."

Octopuses may live five or six years, says Cecil Brosseau, retired 14 director of Point Defiance Aquarium in Tacoma, Washington. "The male dies six weeks after mating. The female dies after the eggs hatch. This has always been the case in the aquarium. Now we're quite sure this also occurs on the outside. If these animals did continue to live for years and years, they would become monstrous. They would all weight 1,000 pounds—or more."

The octopus's growth rate depends partly upon temperament. If 15 an animal is very shy and seldom ventures from its den to eat, it grows slowly. If food is plentiful and it is aggressive, it grows enormously. Brosseau once had a 69-pound octopus that increased to 109 pounds within nine months.

16     Brosseau's specialty is helping man and octopus overcome their fear of one another. "It takes a good week to get an octopus to lose its fear of you," says Brosseau. "But people can overcome their fears immediately. They can be deathly afraid of octopuses and within five minutes you teach them not to be. It happens every day. You talk them into touching the animal. Then they play with it. Then they don't want to leave. That's why we display octopuses this way (in open-top tanks)."

17     Embryologist and cytologist John M. Arnold of Kewalo Marine Laboratory in Hawaii claims that octopuses have individual personalities and are quite intelligent. He tells about a little one from the waters off Bimini in the Bahamas to which he started feeding small snails. He gave the octopus six shells each day. It carried them around under its web, eating them one at a time when hungry. Then the little animal learned to pry open Arnold's fingers in search of the snails. To avoid overfeeding it, he sometimes gave it an empty shell. However the octopus soon learned to insert an arm tip into each shell to see if it held anything before bothering to take it.

18     "Some octopuses tend to react differently to different individuals," says Arnold. "I had 14 adult octopuses, each kept in an individual fiber glass laundry tub. Each morning when I came to work the octopuses would sense my footsteps and stick an arm or two through the wire on their tank lids. On the other hand, one woman felt squeamish about octopuses when she first worked in the lab. She declared them to be the ugliest, slimiest things she'd ever seen, and rapped on the sides of their tank. Soon they got to know her. Even after she stopped intentionally annoying them, they squirted water through the tank lids whenever she walked by. No one else in the laboratory evoked such a response."

19     The animal is not only clever, it is also diligent. The female common octopus, says F. G. Wood, a former curator at Marineland of Florida, is one of the most faithful mothers in the sea. After mating, she returns to her solitary life and produces eggs. Each is about half the size of a grain of rice. As the eggs emerge, she weaves and cements their stems together to form strands up to six inches

long. Then she hangs them under a ledge or in a cave. There may be 1,000 eggs in a strand. One octopus may lay as many as 325,000 eggs in two weeks.

During the two to four more weeks it takes the eggs to hatch, the  20
mother octopus cares for them without pause. From the moment she starts nesting, she refuses food and repels intruders. She blows water on the strands and runs her arms through them to aerate the eggs. When they hatch, her job is done. She dies.

Octopuses may have acquired their bad name by being mistaken  21
for the quick-to-bite squid, a close relative. But the octopus's beak and venom are for its natural prey. Only the small (average size is four inches) blue-ringed octopus of Australia is very poisonous to man. In the last twenty-five years, it has caused six injuries and three deaths. But even this octopus does its best to stay away from people in the first place.

Photographer-writer Valerie Taylor was once taking stills in Port  22
Hacking near Sydney "when I saw a common octopus in the entrance to a small cave. He tried to blow my camera away with jets of water, then tried pushing with his arms. All his efforts were concentrated on the camera. He seemed to ignore the huge creature attached. Finally he pushed the camera to the edge of a drop-off and with one final effort heaved it over. Once he moved away from his cave I noticed a second octopus inside, probably a female." Taylor has gently handled the blue-ringed octopus many times. She finds it does its utmost to avoid contact with people, just as other species do.

Taylor, like everyone who is familiar with the octopus, finds it to  23
be not a gruesome monster of the deep, but an intelligent creature with a distinct, even lovable character.

# Think about:

1.  the main characteristics of octopuses that the writer brings out in the article.

2.  some of the most interesting supporting examples the writer provides for each of these characteristics.

3.  some differences between the picture Pratt-Johnson presents of octopus life and the picture most people have of these mollusks.

4.  the different kinds of octopuses. What facts do you remember about how large and how small different octopuses are and about where the different species live and how they care for their needs?

# Write about:

an animal you feel is misunderstood. Correct the false impressions many people have about cats, ostriches, sheep, wolves, a particular breed of dog, or some other creature.

# Try out:

finding at least one book or magazine article as a source of information that adds to what you already know about the animal. First, list the things you think you know about the animal that contradict what many people believe. Next, list some questions you have. Then, when you read the book or article, take brief notes on material that answers your questions, or that corrects a previous impression of yours. Use your own words to summarize points the author makes. Pay particular attention to finding some direct quotations that will add authority to your report. Then, in writing your paper, try working these quotations into paragraphs of your own writing. Note the way that Pratt-Johnson does this in ¶¶ 1, 11, 13, 16, and 22, for example. Put basic information about the source, including the number of the page on which you found the quotation, in parentheses after each quotation.

# PERSUASION

*Selection Twenty-Nine*

*Why Have Children? A Talk Is Left Up in the Air*

## Look for:

1.    the main difference of opinion between the writer and the passenger sitting next to him on the plane.

2.    the two questions the other passenger asks. How did these questions help the writer to shape his own thoughts?

3.    these words:
   **protracted (proh-TRACT-ed)—lengthy, spelled out in some detail** [1]

   **taut (TAWT)—stretched tight** [2]

   **lawyerly (LAW-yer-lee)—with the manner of a lawyer** [7]

   **abstract (ab-STRACT)—opposite of concrete, referring to ideas rather than to things you can get your hands on** [10]

   **continuum (kun-TIN-you-um)—something continuous and all of a piece; here, the whole timespan of the human race** [12]

   **deplaned (dee-PLAYND)—got off the plane. (The prefix "de"—Latin word for "from"—signals "away from.")** [16]

# Why Have Children? A Talk Is Left Up in the Air

Edward M. White

It was one of those protracted intimate conversations possible only 1
between perfect strangers. She, in the airplane window seat, was a
young attorney. I, next to her by chance, a middle-aged writer and
teacher. The subject was children.

"All the social pressures!" she was saying. She and her physician 2
husband had decided not to have children. The decision was a tense
and uncomfortable one, as her taut lips and twisting fingers showed.
She wanted arguments, good arguments, not social pressures. My
wife and I have five children, with an occasional foster child; I
proposed myself as an expert in the pains and pleasures of parenthood.

"I'd do it again, if I could go back," I said. "But not now, not 3
more," I hastened to add. "Not at this age."

She smiled at my reservations, nodding. We summed up easily the 4
most obvious arguments against having children: the loss of freedom,
the expense, the worry, the inevitability of disappointed expecta-
tions. The schools: integration, disintegration; neighborhoods; play
areas; the drug culture, the counterculture, the TV culture, and so
on, and on. Most centrally, the need to put yourself second in life,
at least on some occasions.

"But why *not* be self-centered?" she said. Why not indeed? How 5
was I to argue against this newfangled virtue, looking forward as I
was to the lack of responsibility just ahead as my children leave home
for college.

"But look at the advantages you could give to your children," I 6
struck out, lamely.

"That's only a reason for someone already convinced," she re- 7
turned, lawyerly. "What is that to me?"

"Besides," I went on, "you know how insensitive and selfish the 8
childless become as they age. Children keep you young, human."

"Oh sure. Next you'll tell me that suffering is good for the soul." 9

From *Los Angeles Times,* January 14, 1980. Reprinted by permission of the author.

10    We stopped the abstract talk. The only logical arguments for having children are social, not personal, and we had agreed that social arguments are not personally convincing. We hung there, in the air, seeking some emotional logic, not sure where it was. Her tone softened.

11    "Why did you have children?"

12    Love had something to do with it, I knew, but I couldn't quite say how. Quite simply, I like kids in general, and mine in particular. But there is something selfish in my love for my children. They somehow help me fit into time. Perhaps that was it, finally: Without children we are flashes in pans; with them we belong on Earth, with a future and hence with a past. Our children put us in the continuum.

13    We talked of parents, then: mine close, hers distant.

14    "You must feel very much alone," I said.

15    "We are all alone," she replied. The flight was over.

16    We both smiled and shrugged as we unbuckled our seat belts, knowing that reasons are finally afterthoughts on family matters, and well aware that we would never see each other again. We shouldered our suitcases and deplaned. She headed purposefully toward the rental cars, and I turned to where my family was waiting.


## Think about:

1.    the arguments on the other passenger's side. Why does White list arguments that oppose his own position?

2.    what the writer and the lawyer agreed on concerning arguments on the topic they were discussing. Could either one have convinced the other that his or her position was "right" or "wrong"? Why or why not?

3.    the writer's feeling of satisfaction with his choice of a way of life. What does he mean by stating that, because of his children, he feels like "part of the continuum"? Is this point —whether you agree with him or not—a good one in favor of his position? Why or why not?

4.   the lawyer's statement "We are all alone." What does she mean by this? What does White say that suggests he finds a difference between the way she is alone and the way he is? What does he imply about future aloneness for each of them?

5.   the tone of this essay (see pp. 15 and 118 on *tone*). Is the tone angry and urgent? Calm and thoughtful? Concerned? Controlled? Grim? Accepting? Joyous? What kind of reader is likely to be persuaded to White's point of view? What readers will not? In either case, how does White's tone in this essay help to make his point of view clear?

## Write about:

a personal decision you have made because you feel it is right for you. Give reasons for choosing this course of action. Indicate some reasons another person might decide differently. Be sure to stress why you think your choice is right for you rather than why others ought to share your opinion. You might write about decisions such as to marry or to stay single, to qualify yourself for a particular occupation, to work and attend college at the same time, to join—or to stay away from—a particular church, club, gang, fraternity, political party, or other organization.

## Try out:

establishing the tone you want to use to tell your reader something you are doing in your life that makes sense to you in your circumstances. In this kind of essay, you will be explaining, not selling, an idea. Although you may have met opposition from other people who wanted you to make a different decision, remember that the reader you want to reach is not an opponent but someone who is trying to understand you and your position. By your tone, you will show the readers that your intent is not to make them do what you are doing but to help them understand why you are doing it.

In order to establish the tone you want and to make your explanation clear to the reader, try writing your essay in the form of a conversation, as White does. This conversation will be between you and someone who may take a different position on the subject you have chosen. This written conversation may be recorded to some extent as an actual conversation taking place between you and another person. Or you can write down your own thoughts and opinions and write what another person you know (a friend? a parent? a teacher? a public official? a boss or coworker?) would probably say if you got him or her into a conversation on this topic.

You can probably use an organization and method of development much like White's. Note that White begins by setting the scene—that is, by showing where and when the conversation he writes about took place. Then, when he gets into the conversation, he moves directly from one person's speech to the other person's speech without leaving the reader in doubt about which one is speaking. (See pp. 21 and 132 on writing *dialogue*.) Note that occasionally he summarizes views instead of writing down exactly everything that is said. And, finally, he sums up his own point of view in ¶ 12 (after apparently having thought it through during the conversation). You will want to pay particular attention to the summing up part of your paper because in it you are most likely to win the understanding of your audience.

*What's Our Image? A Look At Black Films*

# Look for:

1.      the problem Shelton brings up in the first paragraph and the general solution she proposes in the last paragraph.

2.      the writer's detailed analysis of the problem and her explanation of its existence.

3.      these words:
        **condescending (con-dee-SEND-ing)—with an attitude that makes another person feel put down, looked down on** [5]
        **dearth (DERTH)—scarcity** [8]
        **substantive (SUB-stan-tiv)—full of substance, meaningful, substantial, having "something *to* it"** [8]

# What's Our Image? A Look At Black Films

Suzanne Shelton

1    Why are most "black" films so boring? Either I'm subjected to watching black men pimp, shoot up, beat up, and cut up or I'm asked to identify with the "simple" folk who seldom exhibit conflicting feelings or goals, and who, most often, are portrayed as helpless victims. The writer and directors tug on my heart strings; I cry buckets of tears but still I leave the theatre unsatisfied. And, let us not forget the newest wave of black films—much like their white counterpart—which invariably shows a group of grown men "palling" around, getting in trouble, and oops! getting caught. Comedy.

2    Black films seem to fall into very few categories. There's comedy, there's the "action" film where the screen is littered with bodies and hypodermics; there's the "family" film or "see how we've suffered," and finally there's the "inspirational" film, better known as "if he can do it, I can do it." But where are the parts for actors and actresses of stature? Cicely Tyson, Beah Richards, and Rosalind Cash come immediately to mind. Black actors seem to fare better in this case, more often getting parts which have broad and deep characterizations, and having opportunities to work with international directors. But black women most often are cast as mothers or prostitutes—that is, if the role is more than a walk on.

3    Primarily I'm dissatisfied because I'm shown nothing larger than myself. No questions have been posed that are larger than my everyday life. As a result, the black film industry has become bogged down in "entertainment." Now, there's nothing wrong with entertainment. It's just that that shouldn't be all of it.

4    So the question arises—are the plays and screenplays not being written? Are there no black writers out there dealing with those eternal, universal, and human questions? Why have there been so

few adaptations of the brilliant black novels published in the last 40 years? One would think that black people never feel confused or lost, wonder about the purpose of this life, ponder cause and effect, or our own unique identity. Not all of us look to the Bible, mama, or the needle for the answers. If I believed all I saw in these films as representative of black people, I'd think we only feel and react. We never think.

There are too few plays and movies where we leave touched by 5 questions which embrace all humanity. It's a very condescending attitude on the part of producers, writers, and directors that says: "make 'em laugh, make 'em cry—that's enough." Well, it's not enough and it's time we said so. The important political, social, and spiritual questions that are arising in this country are being addressed by others and not by ourselves. If we're so busy laughing and crying (kinda like slavery times, Massah), we'll be drying the tears from our eyes when the changes happen. Then it'll be too late.

So when people talk to me about a "Renaissance of Black Film," 6 I say Bah! Humbug! Pablum! As poisonous to us as white sugar! Are there exceptions? Of course. But too few of them.

Where are our great thinkers—those who are willing to peel back 7 the surface of things and look below? I believe they're out there but they're not getting heard; and they're not getting heard because the people with the money—black and white—aren't willing to listen and take a chance. Which brings me to the reason for this entire discussion.

Where are the black backers? There are enough black people 8 walking around this city investing money in movies, theatre, and other forms of entertainment that there is no excuse for such a dearth of good, substantive film and theatre art. The cynic says: "It's unprofitable. This is a business." I say they should see the number of black and Third World people filling the audiences of so-called "art" houses. The interest in foreign films is clearly growing. Here's a ready-made market that's sure to increase. If filmmakers would show strong, thinking, active individuals on the screen, they'd have no problem securing an audience from any sector. For years we've been complaining that not all black people are alike, yet everytime I go to a movie or turn on the tube, the characters are as interchange-able as checker pieces with the shuffling, fuzzy-minded images we rejected years ago.

9     So, am I suggesting a boycott of black films? No. The film industry, such as it is, is still too fragile for that. But I do suggest that a
few letters of complaint sent to producers, writers, and directors
might put a little pressure where it's needed. After all, they keep
telling us they're giving us what we want. If we tell them what we
want, loudly and clearly, and we continue to get more of the same,
well. . . .

## Think about:

1.     the *stereotypes* of black people that Shelton says most black
       films today project. When characters in fiction—or real-life
       people—are treated as **stereotypes,** they are not regarded
       as individuals but rather as representations of traits that
       some people attribute to all members of a group. That is,
       they are treated as if cast from a mold or cut out with a
       cookie cutter. What kinds of people does this writer feel
       most of the characters in black films turn out to be?

2.     the stereotype of the black people *in audiences* that must be
       in the minds of most writers, directors, and producers, ac-
       cording to Shelton. What kind of reaction does she say these
       people are trying to get from audiences?

3.     the kinds of films about black people the writer thinks
       should be produced.

4.     the justification she gives for believing that these films
       would be successful.

# Write about:

a *stereotype* you are aware of in TV programs or movies or both. Demonstrate that in these shows characters who are members of a particular group usually turn out to be a certain kind of person. The stereotype of cowboys wearing black hats (or white ones) is an obvious example, but you will think of others. Contrast the generalization you think movies or TV programs are making about doctors, police officers, Chicanos, Germans, fathers, teenagers, or whatever group you have chosen with what you know about real-life individuals who are members of this group.

# Try out:

first, writing down in rough note form a description of the movie or TV stereotype you are dealing with. Include both the physical characteristics and the personality traits that come to your mind when you think of TV or movie doctors, police officers, Chicanos, or _____. Next, to be sure you are being fair to the filmmakers, list some specific movies or TV programs you remember in which portrayals of the kind of person you are writing about fit the stereotype you have described. (If you can't think of several examples, you probably need to choose a different group of people.) Then, list several individuals you have known who belong to the category you are treating but who do not fit the movie or TV stereotype. Note the ways in which they do not fit the stereotype.

When you write, these lists will provide you with a way of contrasting the stereotype with the reality. For example, if you list several TV program doctors who are tall, good-looking, calm, and tactful, and then think of several doctor-acquaintances who aren't like that in appearance and personality—let's say at least one is a peppery little guy—you can easily work into your paper this evidence that the stereotype is not true. Note that Shelton treats the stereotypes in the first part of her essay and then turns to reality.

Warning: The tendency to generalize without enough evidence is a fault any writer may fall into when writing to persuade, as you will be doing here. Because you are dealing with stereotypes, which are a kind of generalization, be careful not to generalize too much yourself. As you probably noticed, Shelton handles this problem by pointing out exceptions.

*Selection Thirty-One*

*You Gave Us Your Dimes*

# Look for:

1.  the problem the author is writing about.

2.  the evidence he gives to show that the situation he is discussing is a serious problem.

3.  Hillam's overall solution to the problem. Note especially the way the last sentence in the essay reinforces the idea implied by the title.

4.  these words:
    **incompetence (in-COM-p'-tenss)—inability to function adequately** [8]
    **inalienable (in-ALE-yen-uh-b'l)—not able to be separated or taken away** [9]
    **compatible (com-PAT-ih-b'l)—working well together, seeming to belong together, getting along** [9]
    **preoccupation (pree-ahk-you-PAY-shun)—exclusive concern** [9]
    **recipient (ree-SIP-ee-ent)—one who receives** [10]
    **intermittently (in-ter-MITT-ent-lee)—now and then** [11]
    **consternation (con-stir-NAY-shun)—confusion, panic** [12]

# You Gave Us Your Dimes

Bruce P. Hillam

In America today there is a minority that is often forced to  1
segregate itself into special schools if its members are lucky enough
to attend school. These people are denied the use of public transportation and are sometimes made to sit in special areas of restaurants,
if they are served at all. The economic opportunities for members
of this group are minimal. According to the Bureau of the Census,
this minority composes about 9 percent of the general population.

Who is this forgotten and sometimes invisible minority? The  2
nation's more than 20 million physically limited citizens. They go
by many other names: the disabled, the handicapped, the excep-
tional and the shut-in, to name a few. It is a uniquely "equal opportunity" minority. There are members from every race and religion,
both sexes and all ages. Membership can be conferred at birth by
a birth defect, or later by a disease such as multiple sclerosis or
diabetes. Some members join by accident, in a car or on a playing
field, others after heart attacks or strokes suffered while just trying
to keep pace with today's modern life.

I joined when I was 16 years old, fifteen years ago. I woke up a  3
typical teen-ager and by nightfall, after a dive into an eddy pool that
resulted in a broken neck, I was paralyzed from the shoulders down.
After eleven months in various hospitals and rehabilitation centers,
I was ready to go back into society confined to an electrically powered wheelchair. After I graduated from high school, my family and
I found that society had written me off. My disability labeled me
as one of life's losers, and society grudgingly would assume the
burden of providing for my existence.

In the early '60s, society was not especially eager to help a seriously  4
disabled person become self-sufficient and independent. The success
rate was low and the cost was high, so why try? Besides, other

minorities were more vocal and better organized. It took a letter to my congressman before the Department of Vocational Rehabilitation would even respond to my repeated requests for testing, counseling and support. To make a long story short, I was one of the lucky ones who had desire, ambition, intelligence and strong family support. In 1973, I received my Ph.D. degree in mathematics. I now wanted a job. This, to me, was the ticket off welfare and to my own self-respect.

5      But society does not expect or require the non-able-bodied to work. In fact, I was lucky when I went for a job interview if the subject of a job and my qualifications for it ever came up. The interviewer was usually more fascinated by my electrically powered wheelchair. I found out that most companies will not consider an obviously physically disabled person for employment. They were afraid that their insurance rates would go up, or that their plant would not be safe enough, or that the possible effect of the presence of an obviously physically limited person might be to lower the general productivity of his co-workers.

6      The real shock came when I got a job. I was put off welfare and forced to assume all my expenses, including the full cost of a live-in medical attendant-housekeeper. My income had tripled but my standard of living remained the same. The welfare laws do not adequately provide for any period of transition. For me, it was all cold turkey.

7      Society in general is ill-equipped to deal with me. In the last fifteen years, my wheelchair and I have been declared a fire hazard in several theaters. I have been served meals in separate dining areas of restaurants since, as the owners were quick to point out, I might upset the other customers and lessen their enjoyment of the meal. On several occasions, I have been very nearly hit by traffic as I worked my way across the street hoping to find a ramp or driveway onto the sidewalk on the other side.

8      Some people do the damnedest things when I'm around. I am regularly stopped by well-meaning religious fanatics who insist the only reason I am not up and about is that I lack faith in the Lord, or the other type who assure me God has big plans for me and urge patience. The most discouraging thing, though, is that most people equate a serious physical limitation with mental incompetence.

The Declaration of Independence states that everyone has an  9
inalienable right to life, liberty and the pursuit of happiness. Medical
science has provided life, but where is liberty if I cannot cross the
street because of a manmade barrier, the curb? How is my pursuit
of happiness compatible with society's preoccupation with what I
*cannot* do? And how can I pursue happiness if I am excluded from
many of our society's normal social and recreational functions?

What is needed is a civil-rights bill for the physically limited.  10
Racial minorities, women and the aged have this protection. We
need public transportation that is truly public. The physically limited should have the same right to use a subway or a bus as any other
citizen, and the government should pass and enforce workable laws
to make this a reality. We need a welfare system that encourages a
person to seek to attain as much self-sufficiency and independence
as is possible. We need a welfare system that will help a person make
the difficult transition from recipient to worker but that will also be
flexible enough to allow a person to work part-time if he is not
capable of full-time work. We need housing with doors large enough
for a person in a wheelchair to get into the bathroom, and of course,
we need jobs.

Politicians and labor unionists are only intermittently concerned  11
with our unemployment rate. Perhaps the government ought to
encourage industry to hire the handicapped with a tax credit. Slo-
gans haven't worked. Society must realize that we are not objects to
be pitied. Just watch any telethon to see how widespread and de-
meaning this attitude really is. Indeed, I have often wondered where
all of yesterday's poster children have gone and what they are doing
today.

The physically limited are now organizing and lobbying for their  12
rights as the blacks did twenty years ago and the women did ten years
ago. When more physically limited people become visible in public,
maybe the reaction of my freshman calculus class at the beginning
of the fall term will not be one of consternation as I enter the
classroom for the first time, but one of ordinary acceptance.

You gave us your dimes and we lived. Now allow us our dignity.  13

## Think about:

1.    the specific personal experiences Hillam tells about to show the reader the difficulties he had establishing his personal independence and his professional career.

2.    the prejudices and confusions about his handicap that he has had to cope with. What stereotype does he have to deal with? (See p. 179 on *stereotype*.)

3.    the suggestions Hillam makes for improving the quality of life for physically limited citizens.

4.    the direct, almost conversational style in which this essay is written. Note, for example, the use of a sentence fragment toward the beginning of paragraph 2. Does this usage seem appropriate? Why or why not? Find some additional sentences in which Hillam sounds as if he is *talking* to the reader. Is the style of these sentences appropriate to the subject matter? Why or why not?

## Write about:

your experience with discrimination as a member of a minority group. This group may be ethnic or religious or it may be a group classified according to some other condition or circumstance—perhaps sex or age. (If no other minority classification fits you, you have at least been a student.) As Hillam does, show how what you had to cope with was both objectionable to you and unnecessary as well. Persuade your readers to help bring about more consideration for the group of people you are writing about.

## Try out:

noting experiences that you, as a member of a minority group, had to cope with and found intolerable. Then, when you write your paper, you can work these experiences into the body of your paper as support for your thesis, the way Hillam does. (Note that Hillam's essay does not include a one-sentence statement of his thesis; instead, all of the sentences of the first two paragraphs together state that thesis.)

You will find that "You Gave Us Your Dimes" can serve as a good model for the use of *appropriate language in argument*. You have seen how important factual language is in descriptive writing and in exposition (see "The House," p. 23, and "The Internal Combustion Engine," p. 98, for example). It is just as important in persuasive writing. And in persuasive writing it is always necessary to resist the temptation to let your emotions sidetrack you from the facts. (When this happens, you may appear to "rant and rave.") However, emotional language is appropriate in persuasion when it is necessary to express genuine feeling in order to make a problem clear to the reader. You will notice that Hillam does sometimes use emotional language to express strong feeling. For example, at one point he writes, "Some people do the damnedest things. . . ." (¶ 8) as he tells about the way people annoy him in public places. Another time he shows that he is disturbed at being treated as what he calls "one of life's losers" (¶ 3). But he goes on to use factual language to show how he got himself beyond this label.

Note the way Hillam uses factual language in paragraph 7 to describe situations that would surely be emotion-arousing for anyone. Here he simply reports these situations without comment—except for the terse observation, "Society in general is ill-equipped to deal with me." See if you can use factual language most of the time—as this writer does. You will surely get your reader's attention and support more effectively this way than by letting yourself go with howls of woe and rage. Use emotional language sparingly—that is, do not use it so much that you lose your reader's respect or confidence.

How Sports Can Hurt Your Child

# Look for:

1.  the writer's general answer to the question implied by her title—that is, look for her *thesis.*

2.  specific, factual evidence Pascoe provides to support her thesis.

3.  these words:
    **grievance (GREE-vanss)—complaint about an injustice**
    [2]
    **fervor (FER-v'r)—passion** [2]
    **relegate (RELL-uh-gate)—push away, or off, to an unimportant position** [3]
    **orthopedic (or-tho-PEE-dick)—having to do with treatment of bones and joints** [3]

# How Sports Can Hurt Your Child

Elizabeth Jean Pascoe

The West Springfield (Massachusetts) Hockey Association was    1
having another championship season last winter. But in the locker
room it was civil war. Some of the players had quit and their parents
were consulting lawyers about the terms of the youngsters' releases,
which allowed them to play for other teams. What was at stake?
Athletic scholarships? A chance to play with the pros? Nothing like
that. This was Pee Wee hockey, and the players were only eight to
ten years old. Some of their parents were simply miffed that their
sons had been assigned to the scrub team instead of the first string.

The West Springfield parents may have carried their grievance to    2
ridiculous lengths, but the fervor with which they involved themselves in their sons' competitive sports is not unique. All across the
country competitive sports for elementary-school children have become serious business. From Little League baseball, parents have
gone on to organize football, lacrosse, soccer, basketball and hockey
leagues for children as young as six years old. And just as in Little
League, the emphasis is on winning—all the way. Sadly, one of the
most important points of children's sports—body development—is
being lost to many children who don't quickly emerge as "winners."

There's nothing wrong with winning, but children under 12 need    3
to learn to *enjoy* participating in sports. That means mastering body
skills such as running, jumping, throwing, hitting, catching and
kicking a ball. Much of their ability to do this depends on the stage
of physical and intellectual development they are in. Those who
mature early and are coordinated will shine; those who develop
slowly may get pegged as unathletic. Competitive sports—especially
when parents have a big stake in them—tend to make superstars out
of the children who play well and relegate the slow and the awkward

to the bench. Instead of learning to enjoy and participate in sports, these children become the spectators of later years, while for the superstars winning becomes a matter of excessive team spirit. Some are pushed so hard to maintain their team's winning streak that they actually do themselves harm. Dr. Maurice Cowen, an orthopedic surgeon in New York, says that he frequently treats youngsters whose shoulders or elbows have been injured from pitching too often in one game. Little League players are limited to pitching six innings a week no matter how many games are scheduled. Still, some children overextend themselves despite the rule.

4     "A little competition is okay," says one grade-school physical-education teacher, "but not so much that losing is a disaster. At this age, what kids need is the experience of taking part in a sport, even if they're not very good at it. After all, only about three percent of them will ever become athletes. We don't want the rest to grow up to be just spectators."

5     The selection process for a competitive sport can be cruel, too. "In grade school there's a tremendous need to belong," explains Dr. Marvin Clein, chairman of the University of Denver's department of sports sciences and founder of its Human Performance Laboratory that helps athletes analyze and improve their performance under stress. "At that age, being rejected for a team can amount to total rejection. Parents' involvement can also be devastating. The children don't participate because *they* want to; they do it for the coach or for their parents. Then, when they fail to win, they feel a terrible guilt because they have let somebody down. That's probably the single biggest reason that children get discouraged and quit a sport."

6     Grade-school children may suffer an additional drawback under such pressure: Many haven't developed the physical attributes necessary to play team sports that were designed for adults. Take, for example, baseball. "One factor that influences batting skill is the ability to track the ball from pitcher to home plate with the eyes," says Professor Don Morris of Montana State University. Dr. Morris has made a study of the skills necessary to play team sports and the stages of physical development that children need to complete before they can play them successfully. "Up to age six, children can track a ball only as it moves horizontally. From six to seven and a half, they can track a ball that's moving vertically or horizontally, but

if it's moving in an arc they probably won't be able to follow it visually until they are eight or eight and a half."

He found that if children are allowed to make up or change the rules of a game, they tend to design a game in which most of them are successful most of the time. Morris believes that one way to improve sports participation for grade schoolers is to change the way sports are played, to adapt games to the physical development of the youngsters and concentrate on teaching them game-playing skills and taking responsibility for their own actions. "Many people resist this kind of approach," he says. "They feel that when you change the rules of a game like baseball, you're changing an American tradition." 7

But some elementary schools are using his methods. At Denver's Swansea elementary school, for instance, children play no team sports until they reach third grade, and then it may be only a simplified form of football in which there are no running moves, just throwing and catching the ball. Or they may play kickball—a version of baseball in which the "pitcher" rolls a soccer ball toward the plate and the "batter" kicks it—which allows them to practice the skills of kicking, catching, throwing and rolling a ball while learning the rules of softball. Younger children spend their gym classes working out on ropes and mats, learning to handle balls, moving in rhythms and playing circle, line and tag games in which they can practice body skills and movements. "We talk about manners and sportsmanship," says one of the school's physical-education teachers, Gene Yost. "If we keep score in a game, we trade the kids around so that everybody is on a winning or losing team at some time." And in the process the children learn that they can all participate in sports with reasonable competence even if they aren't superstars. 8

Dr. Clein of the University of Denver adds, "There is no place where every child can learn the lessons of life better than on an athletic team. The coach of a children's team has a very big responsibility. He or she can be a teacher and turn the experience into a situation where children learn values as well as athletic skills. But if the emphasis is strictly on winning, the coach becomes a manager, telling the kids to go faster and push harder. There's nothing wrong with winning as one objective, but the overriding objective should be educational." 9

10    Montana State University's Don Morris adds, "Rather than spending thousands of dollars for traditional sports for a select group of children, we should make the dollars available to recreation programs in which all children can participate. I dream of the day when people are willing to change the games children play in ways that allow children of all abilities to play within one game structure. When this concept is realized, then we will have truly returned the games to the children."

## Think about:

1.    the point Pascoe makes about adults overemphasizing competition among children. What evidence does she give to support her position? What kind of evidence is it? Do you find this evidence convincing?

2.    the alternative Pascoe suggests to the emphasis on competition in children's sports. What does she think is more important than "winning"? Why?

## Write about:

your opinion of how physical education—in the broadest sense, including general health-building—should be improved for people of any age you choose. The kind of experience in body development you suggest may be in or out of school and may be planned by an organization or by an individual acting alone. Persuade your readers that what you advocate is a useful approach for many people. If you wish, contrast your suggested approach with what is provided by conventional school or community programs. Or, if you prefer, explain and defend an existing program (for example, the Police Athletic League or your high school's or college's varsity sports program).

# Try out:

using Pascoe's essay as a model for the organization of your persuasive paper. Note that this writer uses an organizational pattern that you are at least partly familiar with. She begins with an *introduction* (a rather long one) to attract the reader's attention and interest; this introduction includes a direct statement of her *thesis*—the last sentence in her second paragraph. Then she proceeds to support her thesis in *body paragraphs* and to wind up with a paragraph which reinforces her original thesis statement. The difference between the way this organization is used here and the way it is used in earlier sections of the book is that Pascoe is writing an *argument,* that is, she is persuading people to accept her position on a particular issue. Therefore, the body of her essay consists of paragraphs in which she gives evidence to support her thesis: quotations from authorities, her own knowledge of the way children develop, and examples of abuses of children under the system she is criticizing. You will probably not need quotations because you will take a subject about which you have ideas based upon your personal experience. But be sure to give specific evidence of some sort to support every point you make in your argument.

## Judges—The New Ruling Class

# Look for:

1.     the answer to the question implied by the title. In what way —and to what extent—are judges, according to Kerby, a "ruling class"?

2.     specific evidence the writer presents to back up his argument.

3.     suggestions that the writer advances for correcting the practices he criticizes.

4.     these words:

       **media (MEED-ee-uh)**—means of getting something to someone. "Media" is the plural of the word "medium." As used in this selection and as widely used today, "media" means methods of communication —especially television and newspapers. [1]

       **mandarins (MAN-d'-rinz)**—ancient Oriental lords with powers of life or death over their subjects [2]

       **magisterial (madge-uh-STEER-ee-ull)**—authoritative, having the characteristics of a master or teacher. From the Latin word *magister* (master) which also gives us the word "magistrate." [4]

       **jurists (JURR-ists)**—judges (not to be confused with jurors) [4]

       **denigrate (DEN-ih-grate)**—put down verbally, deny importance to [11]

       **substantive (SUB-stan-tiv)**—large, of some substance and, in this context, far-reaching [11]

       **tirade (TY-rade)**—ranting, angry, insulting talk [12]

       **defamation (deh-fam-A-shun)**—speaking ill of someone, taking away a person's "fame," that is, his or her good name [12]

       **mortality (more-TAL-ih-tee)**—the condition of being mortal, that is, alive but destined to die (shared by all living organisms). The root of this word, *mort,* is from Latin; it means "death." [15]

# Judges—The New Ruling Class

Phil Kerby

If I ever had any doubts before, I have none now, after attending  1
a conference in Los Angeles over the past weekend on "The Media
and the Law."

Judges are the mandarins of American society.  2

Presidents, Congress, the state legislatures may propose. Judges  3
dispose.

The immediate topic of the conference—graced by the magiste-  4
rial presence of several eminent jurists—was the present conflict
between the courts and the press. The dispute is serious enough to
warrant the attention it is receiving.

The New Jersey courts, without even granting a news reporter a  5
hearing on the merits of his legal defense, clapped him in jail for
refusing to surrender all the information he collected in an investigation of a series of deaths in a New Jersey hospital.

The courts have approved surprise raids by police of newspaper  6
and broadcasting offices, and this ruling also applies to private
homes.

The courts have decided that the government, without notice to  7
a publication, may examine the records of all telephone calls into and
out of a publication's office or that of a broadcast station.

In an offhand opinion, not related to the case at hand, Supreme  8
Court Justice Byron White approved secret trials, if necessary, he
said, "to assure a defendant a fair trial . . ." A secret trial in America?

Yet the broader question—which includes the press-court contro-  9
versy but extends far beyond it—is the revolutionary expansion of
judicial power in recent decades. Whether one agrees or disagrees
with the way this power has been used, it cannot be disputed that
the courts have worked profound changes in our social structure.

10    Since 1954, the school system of the United States has been reorganized under court decisions. The Supreme Court's reapportionment decisions have reorganized the political structures of the states. A federal judge assumed the management of the schools of a large city. Another federal judge assumed control of state prisons. A third decided that the welfare program in the state in which he sits was under his jurisdiction and ruled that the state cannot impose any residence requirement upon welfare recipients.

11    Such matters of public policy have fallen into the hands of the courts because, said one legal commentator, of the "inability of the political process to meet basic problems in our society." That is true to a considerable extent, but power feeds upon power, and unchecked authority, wisely used in one instance, may be abused in the next. The late Justice Hugo Black, not a man to denigrate the role of the judiciary, said in one dissenting opinion that some court decisions were "a blank check to alter the meaning of the Constitution as written so as to add to it substantive constitutional changes which a majority of the court at any time believes are needed to meet present-day problems."

12    Notions of infallibility and boundless authority are not the least dangers posed by the extension of judicial power into every nook and corner of the nation's life. How else can one explain federal Judge Frederick Lacey's tirade directed at the New York Times reporter who, citing the Constitution and the New Jersey shield law, declined to surrender his notes? While berating the reporter and mangling the truth, Judge Lacey knew that he himself was protected by an iron-clad, defamation-proof shield just recently reinforced by the Supreme Court.

13    Some judges, when confronted with a claim of privilege under the First Amendment, are fond of asserting that no principle is absolute, that the First Amendment must be balanced against other constitutional values. But in the bizarre case of an Indiana judge, the Supreme Court did discover one absolute—absolute immunity for judges. "A judge," said Justice White, "is absolutely immune from liability for his judicial acts," and that applies even though a judge acts beyond his authority or with malice. The judge in question, without a hearing or notice or appointment of anyone to represent a 15-year-old girl, ordered her sterilized under the pretext she was having her appendix removed.

Judges off the bench, as I noted at the conference, are much like 14
other people. They sometimes falter at a question, miss the point,
become confused, veer off on a tangent and in other ways behave
quite normally, which arouses my sympathy.

In respect to the most powerful branch of the system, the federal 15
judiciary, should judges be burdened with such great power for a
lifetime? Or should we lighten their oppressive duties by limiting
their appointments to a term long enough to grant them independence from the pressures of the moment but short enough to remind
them of their mortality?

## Think about:

1.   the writer's main idea. Where does he state it directly? Do
     you agree that the incidents he tells about are abuses of
     power?

2.   the writer's journalistic style of paragraphing. This article
     originally appeared as a newspaper column, and, as you
     learned earlier, newspaper writers often write very short
     paragraphs as a way of grabbing readers' attention. Note,
     for example, that Kerby's thesis statement ("Judges are the
     mandarins of American society.") is placed in a separate
     paragraph. A more conventional arrangement is:

     > If I ever had any doubts before, I have none now, after
     > attending a conference in Los Angeles over the past week-
     > end on "The Media and the Law": Judges are the mandar-
     > ins of American society.

     Where else in the article do you find unconventional para-
     graphing?

3.      the organization of "Judges—The New Ruling Class." It is somewhat different from that of any other selection you have read so far. For that reason it will be a good idea to reread the article with a pencil in hand, making sure that you follow the writer's development of his main idea.

     Note that after stating his thesis, Kerby lists some recent court decisions he thinks were wrong. Number these decisions in the margin as you come to them and be sure you understand what problems all these decisions are concerned with. In ¶ 9 the writer restates his thesis as he speaks of "the revolutionary expansion of judicial power in recent decades." Why does he do this? In the body of the article, which begins with ¶ 10, he gives examples to support his thesis. Number these examples as you read them. Which portion of the article serves as the conclusion? What suggestions does Kerby make in his conclusion for improving the situation he is writing about?

## Write about:

     the dangers of misuse of power by persons in some position of authority. Such people could be: parents, teachers, coaches, police officers, city councilmen, senators, employers, shop foremen, or office managers. You may have to look up some information on the legal rights and duties now in effect for a person in the position you are writing about. Your examples of possible abuse of power could include incidents from your own personal experience, from newspaper items, or from situations your common sense tells you may arise from abuse of power. But be sure to make clear when you are presenting facts and when you are just speculating. Choose, as Kerby has, a topic you feel strongly about. And, as he does, control the language you use to express your feeling. In this way, you will persuade your readers to consider the reasonableness of your argument (see p. 186 on *emotional* versus *factual language* and appropriate uses of language to express feeling).

# Try out:

before you write, making two lists, side by side. The first will be a list of duties that are required or expected of people in the position you are writing about; the second will be a list of things that go wrong or could go wrong when people in authority usurp—that is, take—more power over others than they have a right to.

Then, when you write, draw from these lists to tell what should and should not be done by a person in this position. Limit your criticism to comments on excessive or unreasonable exercise of power. Be sure to have enough examples to support your thesis, as Kerby does. And decide on appropriate ways of catching your readers' interest in your introduction, of providing evidence in the body of your paper, and of tying your argument together in your conclusion.

*Prayer Before Birth*

# Look for:

1.  the identity of the speaker of the poem. Note the repetition of the first phrase.

2.  the separate plea in each of the stanzas as the speaker asks to be heard, consoled, and so forth.

3.  the strong and unusual rhythm of this poem. As you read it aloud (to yourself or to a friend), why not pretend that *you* are the speaker and try to persuade your audience to do as you ask or at least to care about your cause. (Don't worry, especially in the first reading, if you do not understand the meaning of every phrase the poet uses.)

4.  these words:
    **stoat (STOTE)—weasel** [2]

    **ghoul (GOOL)—an imaginary evil creature (said to haunt graveyards and feed on corpses)** [3]

    **console (con-SOLE)—sympathize with *and* give help to** [4]

    **dandle (DAN-d'l)—to rock, bounce, play with** [9]

    **hector (HECK-t'r)—nag, bother, hassle** [20]

    **folly (FAH-lee)—foolishness** [22]

    **dragoon (draa-GOON)—kidnap for the purpose of forcing the person to work or to do something against his or her will** [30]

    **lethal (LEE-th'l)—deadly, possessing the power to kill** [30]

    **automaton (aw-TOM-uh-tahn)—anything that reacts automatically, that is, without reasoning or feeling** [30]

# Prayer Before Birth

### Louis MacNeice

I am not yet born; O hear me.
Let not the bloodsucking bat or the rat or the stoat or the
   club-footed ghoul come near me.

I am not yet born, console me.
I fear that the human race may with tall walls wall me,      5
   with strong drugs dope me, with wise lies lure me,
      on black racks rack me, in blood-baths roll me.

I am not yet born; provide me
With water to dandle me, grass to grow for me, trees to talk
   to me, sky to sing to me, birds and a white light      10
      in the back of my mind to guide me.

I am not yet born; forgive me
For the sins that in me the world shall commit, my words
   when they speak me, my thoughts when they think me,
      my treason engendered by traitors beyond me,      15
         my life when they murder by means of my
            hands, my death when they live me.

I am not yet born; rehearse me
In the parts I must play and the cues I must take when
   old men lecture me, bureaucrats hector me, mountains      20
      frown at me, lovers laugh at me, the white
         waves call me to folly and the desert calls
            me to doom and the beggar refuses
               my gift and my children curse me.
I am not yet born; O hear me,      25

Reprinted by permission of Faber and Faber Ltd. from *The Collected Poems of Louis MacNeice*.

Let not the man who is beast or who thinks he is God
    come near me.

I am not yet born; O fill me
With strength against those who would freeze my
      humanity, would dragoon me into a lethal automaton,
        would make me a cog in a machine, a thing with
          one face, a thing, and against all those
            who would dissipate my entirety, would
              blow me like thistledown hither and
                thither or hither and thither
                  like water held in the
                    hands would spill me.
Let them not make me a stone and let them not spill me.
Otherwise kill me.

## Think about:

1.     the ideas for the better world that the poet implies we should provide. You might list, stanza by stanza, the problems and wishes the poem expresses.

2.     the meaning of stanza 4 (lines 12–17). What is the speaker —that is, the "not yet born" child of the poem—asking to be forgiven for? Who does it (for we do not know its sex yet) suggest will be responsible for its future words and actions? This speaker, according to the poem, will grow up to "speak" and "think" in particular ways and even, possibly, to commit crimes such as "treason" and "murder." What does the speaker say will influence the future development of an unborn child?

3.     the ending. Did you expect this idea? Does it seem right for the poem? Why or why not?

# Write about:

one part of your wishes, hopes, and dreams for the better world you would like your children—or any children—to grow up in. Limit your topic to one particular change you would like to see brought about; your topic might arise from a problem the poem may remind you of—for example, war, pollution, or drug abuse. Try to persuade your reader to accept your point of view by telling what you see going wrong now and what you would like to see happening and being done in the future.

# Try out:

writing this assignment in the form of a personal letter. A letter writer, like a poet, can be primarily concerned with expressing deep personal feeling in a memorable and original way. Write a letter that is to be read fifteen or twenty years from now by someone you have in mind who is now a young child or even an unborn baby. Tell this person specifically what your hope is for the future. Tell what you would like to see accomplished to make his or her experiences better than your own. For this assignment use whatever organization and whatever kind of language seem right for your purpose. But be sure to keep in mind your *audience,* that is, the fifteen- or twenty-year-old person who will be reading your letter. Try to make what you are writing informative, interesting, and emotionally moving.

*I Have a Dream*

# Look for:

1.  the identity of the "great American" to whom the first sentence refers. Where was King standing when he gave this speech? (The location is implied in the first paragraph.)

2.  the main idea of this written speech. Just what does King's "dream" consist of?

3.  these words:

    manacles (MAN-uh-k'lz)—handcuffs (from the Latin *manus*, meaning hand) [2]

    tranquillity (tran-QUILL-ih-tee)—calmness [6]

    militancy (MILL-ih-t'n-see)—readiness to fight [8]

    inextricably (in-EX-trick-uh-blee)—in a way that does not allow one to get untangled or free [8]

    devotees (deh-vote-AZE)—loyal, enthusiastic, devoted followers (a French word) [9]

    tribulations (trib-you-LAY-shunz)—trials, troubles [15]

    redemptive (ree-DEMP-tiv)—allowing for salvation or redemption [15]

    wallow (WAH-lo)—splash and roll about—like a pig in the mud [16]

    oasis (oh-A-sis)—a place with water and vegetation surrounded by a vast area of dry land [20]

    interposition (IN-ter-po-ZISH-un)—the act of getting in between people or things [23]

    nullification (null-ih-f'-KAY-shun)—the act of reducing to nothing; destruction [23]

    prodigious (pro-DIJ-us)—big, huge, enormous [29]

# I Have a Dream

**Martin Luther King, Jr.**

Five score years ago, a great American, in whose symbolic shadow    1
we stand, signed the Emancipation Proclamation. This momentous
decree came as a great beacon light of hope to millions of Negro
slaves who had been seared in the flames of withering injustice. It
came as a joyous daybreak to end the long night of captivity.

But one hundred years later, we must face the tragic fact that the    2
Negro is still not free. One hundred years later, the life of the Negro
is still sadly crippled by the manacles of segregation and the chains
of discrimination. One hundred years later, the Negro lives on a
lonely island of poverty in the midst of a vast ocean of material
prosperity. One hundred years later, the Negro is still languished in
the corners of American society and finds himself an exile in his own
land. So we have come here today to dramatize an appalling condition.

In a sense we have come to our nation's Capital to cash a check.    3
When the architects of our republic wrote the magnificent words
of the Constitution and the Declaration of Independence, they were
signing a promissory note to which every American was to fall heir.
This note was a promise that all men would be guaranteed the
unalienable rights of life, liberty, and the pursuit of happiness.

It is obvious today that America has defaulted on this promissory    4
note insofar as her citizens of color are concerned. Instead of honor-
ing this sacred obligation, America has given the Negro people a bad
check; a check which has come back marked "insufficient funds."
But we refuse to believe that the bank of justice is bankrupt. We
refuse to believe that there are insufficient funds in the great vaults
of opportunity of this nation. So we have come to cash this check
—a check that will give us upon demand the riches of freedom and
the security of justice.

5    We have also come to this hallowed spot to remind America of the fierce urgency of *now*. This is no time to engage in the luxury of cooling off or to take the tranquilizing drug of gradualism. *Now* is the time to make real the promises of democracy. *Now* is the time to rise from the dark and desolate valley of segregation to the sunlit path of racial justice. *Now* is the time to open the doors of opportunity to all of God's children. *Now* is the time to lift our nation from the quicksands of racial injustice to the solid rock of brotherhood.

6    It would be fatal for the nation to overlook the urgency of the moment and to underestimate the determination of the Negro. This sweltering summer of the Negro's legitimate discontent will not pass until there is an invigorating autumn of freedom and equality. Nineteen sixty-three is not an end, but a beginning. Those who hope that the Negro needed to blow off steam and will now be content will have a rude awakening if the nation returns to business as usual. There will be neither rest nor tranquillity in America until the Negro is granted his citizenship rights. The whirlwinds of revolt will continue to shake the foundations of our nation until the bright day of justice emerges.

7    But there is something that I must say to my people who stand on the warm threshold which leads into the palace of justice. In the process of gaining our rightful place we must not be guilty of wrongful deeds. Let us not seek to satisfy our thirst for freedom by drinking from the cup of bitterness and hatred. We must forever conduct our struggle on the high plane of dignity and discipline. We must not allow our creative protest to degenerate into physical violence. Again and again we must rise to the majestic heights of meeting physical force with soul force.

8    The marvelous new militancy which has engulfed the Negro community must not lead us to a distrust of all white people, for many of our white brothers, as evidenced by their presence here today, have come to realize that their destiny is tied up with our destiny and their freedom is inextricably bound to our freedom. We cannot walk alone.

9    And as we walk, we must make the pledge that we shall march ahead. We cannot turn back. There are those who are asking the devotees of civil rights, "When will you be satisfied?"

10    We can never be satisfied as long as the Negro is the victim of the unspeakable horrors of police brutality.

We can never be satisfied as long as our bodies, heavy with the 11
fatigue of travel, cannot gain lodging in the motels of the highways
and the hotels of the cities.

We cannot be satisfied as long as the Negro's basic mobility is 12
from a smaller ghetto to a larger one.

We can never be satisfied as long as a Negro in Mississippi cannot 13
vote and a Negro in New York believes he has nothing for which
to vote.

No, no, we are not satisfied, and we will not be satisfied until 14
justice rolls down like waters and righteousness like a mighty stream.

I am not unmindful that some of you have come here out of great 15
trials and tribulations. Some of you have come fresh from narrow jail
cells. Some of you have come from areas where your quest for
freedom left you battered by the storms of persecution and staggered
by the winds of police brutality. You have been the veterans of
creative suffering. Continue to work with the faith that unearned suffering is redemptive.

Go back to Mississippi, go back to Alabama, go back to South 16
Carolina, go back to Georgia, go back to Louisiana, go back to the
slums and ghettos of our Northern cities, knowing that somehow
this situation can and will be changed. Let us not wallow in the valley
of despair.

I say to you today, my friends, that in spite of the difficulties and 17
frustrations of the moment I still have a dream. It is a dream deeply
rooted in the American dream.

I have a dream that one day this nation will rise up and live out 18
the true meaning of its creed: "We hold these truths to be self-
evident; that all men are created equal."

I have a dream that one day on the red hills of Georgia the sons 19
of former slaves and the sons of former slaveowners will be able to
sit down together at the table of brotherhood.

I have a dream that one day even the state of Mississippi, a desert 20
state sweltering with the heat of injustice and oppression, will be
transformed into an oasis of freedom and justice.

I have a dream that my four little children will one day live in a 21
nation where they will not be judged by the color of their skin but
by the content of their character.

I have a dream today. 22

I have a dream that one day the state of Alabama, whose gover- 23 nor's lips are presently dripping with the words of interposition and nullification, will be transformed into a situation where little black boys and black girls will be able to join hands with little white boys and white girls and walk together as sisters and brothers.

24    I have a dream today.

25    I have a dream that one day every valley shall be exalted, every hill and mountain shall be made low, the rough places will be made plain, and the crooked places will be made straight, and the glory of the Lord shall be revealed, and all flesh shall see it together.

26    This is our hope. This is the faith with which I return to the South. With this faith we will be able to hew out of the mountain of despair a stone of hope. With this faith we will be able to transform the jangling discords of our nation into a beautiful symphony of brotherhood.

27    With this faith we will be able to work together, to pray together, to struggle together, to go to jail together, to stand up for freedom together, knowing that we will be free one day.

28    This will be the day when all of God's children will be able to sing with new meaning, "My country 'tis of thee, sweet land of liberty, of thee I sing. Land where my fathers died, land of the Pilgrims' pride, from every mountainside, let freedom ring."

29    And if America is to be a great nation, this must become true. So let freedom ring from the prodigious hilltops of New Hampshire. Let freedom ring from the mighty mountains of New York. Let freedom ring from the heightening Alleghenies of Pennsylvania!

30    Let freedom ring from the snowcapped Rockies of Colorado! Let freedom ring from the curvaceous peaks of California! But not only that; let freedom ring from Stone Mountain of Georgia! Let freedom ring from Lookout Mountain of Tennessee!

31    Let freedom ring from every hill and molehill of Mississippi. From every mountainside, let freedom ring.

32    When we let freedom ring, when we let it ring from every village and every hamlet, from every state and every city, we will be able to speed up that day when all of God's children, black men and white men, Jews and Gentiles, Protestants and Catholics, will be able to join hands and sing in the words of the old Negro spiritual, "Free at last! Free at last! Thank God Almighty, we are free at last!"

## Think about:

1. specifically what goals for American black people in 1963 King spells out (note especially ¶¶ 9 through 13).

2. warnings King gives about excesses to be avoided (note ¶¶ 7 and 8).

3. the persuasiveness of the language King uses throughout this speech. What metaphors do you find especially effective? (See p. 48 on *metaphor*.) Note particularly ¶¶ 3 and 4 in which several related metaphors are interwoven. Where else does he use repetition besides in the refrain "I have a dream"? Why is this repetition effective?

4. the solid core of fact underlying the emotion that King's language expresses here. What are some of the facts of black experience that King shows his audience that he understands (see ¶¶ 10 to 15)?

## Write about:

something that still urgently needs to be done to bring about better race relations. Be sure to focus on a particular problem, give pertinent facts about it, and, if possible, propose specific actions you think should be taken to correct the problem. For example, you might suggest that your city fund more public parks to provide city residents of various racial backgrounds with appropriate places to relax, exercise, and hold meetings and entertainments. You might recommend that your state revise its system of justice because of the way racial minorities are affected by the present system. You might urge the federal government to guarantee equal opportunity for education by providing funds and guidelines for teachers in inadequate schools. You might urge banks and other private institutions to adopt more liberal lending policies so that more business people from racial minorities can contribute to the economic stability of the country. Or you may think of some other problem, perhaps one that has been on your mind, and suggest a solution—or partial solution—to this problem.

## Try out:

writing your opinion in the form of a letter to the editor of a newspaper. You might go to the library and look over some "Letters to the Editor" columns in any big city newspaper. While you may find some of these letters sketchy or trivial, there will also be some that are well thought out and that can serve as models for you. You will find that the writers of these thoughtful letters have limited themselves to one particular issue which they examine closely, and you should do this too.

You should understand that what you will be doing here is different in certain important respects from what King did in preparing and delivering his famous "I Have a Dream" speech. King was speaking to a group of people most of whom were already sympathetic to his cause. You will be writing to an audience of people with mixed opinions; the only common ground you can assume is an interest in ideas. Therefore you will need to give more specific information to support your basic beliefs than King did. He was a highly skilled public speaker who was a master of techniques for leading a vast audience—physically assembled in front of him—to appropriate emotional as well as intellectual response. You, on the other hand, will be a letter writer putting your own solitary voice on paper to persuade your unknown, unseen readers to agree with your position and perhaps even act upon your suggestions. You will accomplish this through a combination of convincing evidence and appropriate, emotion-arousing language. This emotion-arousing language—like King's—may well include phrases repeated for effect and metaphors carefully chosen to clarify ideas.

In the writing assignment for "Prayer Before Birth" (p. 202), you saw that a *private letter* has something in common with a *poem.* In this assignment, you can see that a *public letter* has something in common with a *speech.* With this public statement you are writing, you will be going on record before your fellow citizens as standing for something. If your letter is published, it may influence other people's opinions in the same way a speech does. It can give you the satisfaction of knowing that your feelings and your knowledge and ideas can influence other people to feel, think, and act—even as Martin Luther King's did.

# Index of Readings and Authors

# To the Student

You, the student, are the final test of the success of our textbooks. We need your reactions and ideas if we are to serve you better. On the following page is a simple questionnaire which, if you would take a few moments to fill it out, will greatly help us to publish more informative and interesting books for you and your instructor.

When completed, simply tear out the page, fold and staple it with the post-paid label showing, and drop it in the mail.

Thank you.

READ TO WRITE
Taylor & Taylor


Your Name (If you wish): _____ Date: _____

School: _____ Your Major: _____

Size of Class: _____

1) What did you like best about this book?

*fold here*

2) What did you like least about this book?


3) Which chapters were easiest for you?  Why?


4) Which chapters were most difficult for you?  Why?


5) In general, how might the book be improved?


May we quote you in our advertising efforts? Yes_____  No_____

Thank you,
Scott, Foresman, College Division

*fold here*

Taylor & Taylor